D1001012

Our Debt to Greece and Rome

EDITORS
GEORGE DEPUE HADZSITS, PH.D.

DAVID MOORE ROBINSON, PH.D., LL.D.

LANGUAGE & PHILOLOGY

ROLAND G. KENT, Ph.D.

COOPER SQUARE PUBLISHERS, INC.
NEW YORK
1963

Published 1963 by Cooper Square Publishers, Inc.
59 Fourth Avenue, New York 3, N.Y.
Library of Congress Catalog Card No. 63-10277

To
MY WIFE

CONTENTS

CONTENTS

LANGUAGE AND PHILOLOGY

LANGUAGE AND PHILOLOGY

I. INTRODUCTION

THE English language, despite its present simplicity of grammatical structure, is of an almost unbelievable complexity in its origins, in fact of a complexity quite unrivaled by any of the better known languages of any period.

The chief sources of our English word-stock are, on the one hand, the Anglo-Saxon speech, and, on the other, the Latin and Greek languages. Yet their relative importance is ill understood by most users of English. Some instructive figures are to be found in the *Literary Digest* for January 25, 1913.[1] In the seventeenth century, George Hickes calculated that nine tenths of our words were of Anglo-Saxon origin; his basis for estimating was the Lord's Prayer. But the sixty-seven words of the Lord's Prayer are hardly adequate for so general a conclusion, though among them are the Latin *debts*, *debtors*, *temptation*, *deliver*, *power*, *glory*, and the Hebrew *amen*. The

English historian Sharon Turner, who died in 1847, estimated that Anglo-Saxon words formed three fifths of the vocabulary and the Norman-French, which is chiefly Latin and Greek, about two fifths. Dean Trench, who died in 1886, made a similar estimate: Anglo-Saxon, 60 percent; Latin, including those received through French, 30 percent; Greek, 5 percent; other sources, 5 percent.

But these estimates lack the weight which can be secured only by examination of the actual words used, every different word being counted once only. Thus the article *the*, which occurs several times in every hundred words, should be counted but once, even though a passage of some thousands of words is considered. The counting of repetitions, it is true, determines the relative frequency of use, as in some recent tabulations to establish the most useful vocabulary of 2000 words for the school child, as a basis of his spelling work.[2] The test revealed that fifty words, much repeated, compose half of all words written; they are the following:

the	*it*	*at*	*dear*	*has*
and	*was*	*we*	*from*	*very*
of	*is*	*on*	*are*	*were*
to	*will*	*he*	*all*	*been*

I	*as*	*by*	*me*	*would*
a	*have*	*but*	*so*	*she*
in	*not*	*my*	*one*	*or*
that	*with*	*this*	*if*	*there*
you	*be*	*his*	*they*	*her*
for	*your*	*which*	*had*	*an*

But these words, despite their frequency, are not half the treasures of our tongue, nor one hundredth; they are utterly empty of content. For example, this list includes only 15 of the 46 different words in the Lord's Prayer, and with the repetitions only 24 of the 67 words. No one could frame even the simplest letter without constantly using words not in this list. In fact, the investigators found that beyond 1000 words they could not draw up an additional list of 1000 words of common use, because the vocabularies of different persons diverged too greatly according to their interests or professions.

Returning to the *Literary Digest*, we find an etymological grouping of nearly 20,000 words of common use in the English-speaking world. We condense it slightly, and get the following:

Words from Anglo-Saxon 3681

Words from German, Dutch, Scandinavian 1359

Words from the same through French	653
Words from Latin direct	2880
Words from Latin, Late Latin, or Romance languages through French	6129
Words from Latin through Provençal	25
Words from Italian, Spanish, Portuguese	228
Words from Greek direct or through Latin	2493
Words from Semitic (Hebrew and Arabic)	371
Words from other languages	654
Hybrid words	675
Words of unknown origin	12
Total	19160

It is rather startling to find that of our vocabulary less than one fifth is by origin Anglo-Saxon, or pure English, and that over three fifths (the fourth to the eighth items, inclusive) come from Latin and Greek. If the table included the rarer words, many of which are familiar to well educated persons, a still higher percentage of Latin and Greek would be found, since almost all technical terms in every field come from those languages, and the rarer words are mainly such technical words.

Not only in vocabulary, but also in word formation, Latin and Greek have exercised an overpowering influence on English; but before discussing these topics, we must first get a reasonable understanding of the interrelations of languages, and of the ways in which they affect one another.

II. LANGUAGE RELATIONSHIP
AND BEHAVIOR

EVERY one familiar with more than one language observes resemblances among them. These resemblances are usually the result not of chance, but of quite different causes. Thus we may compare the words for *seven, ten, father*, in certain modern languages:

Italian	*sette*	*dieci*	*padre*
Provençal	*set*	*detz*	*paire*
French	*sept*	*dix*	*père*
Spanish	*siete*	*diez*	*padre*
Portuguese	*sete*	*dez*	*padre*
Roumanian	*şepte*	*diéce*	. . .

Even hasty consideration convinces the observer that some real connection exists among these various languages, and he will doubtless fancy, quite rightly, that this list could be very greatly extended. It chances that we have the language from which all these words came: it is Latin, where we find *septem, decem, pater*.

One language of the past has lived on, changing in different localities and developing into different dialects, the speakers of which do not without special study understand one another. We might suspect that there are also larger linguistic unities, and that Latin may be merely one of several products of a still earlier unity. Let us examine this table:

English	seven	ten	father
Latin	septem	decem	pater
Greek	ἑπτά	δέκα	πατήρ
Sanskrit	saptá	dáça	pitā̃
Lithuanian	septynì	dēszimt	...

The resemblances here are not so close as in the previous set, yet indicate that these languages are related to each other as are the languages of our first table; but the earlier language, of which these are the later forms, has not come down to us. We infer its existence, however, and name it the *primitive Indo-European language;* by careful examination and comparison of the later languages, we have gained a considerable amount of information about it and its speakers.

This primitive language was spoken long ago, perhaps about 3000 B.C., by a people who lived somewhere between the Baltic Sea and the Black Sea. From time to time, as a result of dissensions, or of overcrowding, or merely of the love

[9]

of wandering, groups or bands set out in various directions. Some reached Persia and India, others spread over Europe; in this volume, we are concerned chiefly with three branches, the Greek, the Italic, and the Teutonic. The Greeks settled in the lands now called Greece, in the neighboring islands, and later in South Italy and Sicily. The Italic tribes occupied most of Italy, where the dialect of Rome and of Latium was known as Latin. The Teutonic tribes covered the greater part of present-day Germany, with extensions into Scandinavia and Britain; their speech has developed into English, German, Dutch, Danish, Swedish, and Norwegian. A fourth branch of the Indo-Europeans, the Celts, occupied France, along with North Italy and a part of Britain.

Details of their history must be left to later chapters; here, let us consider in what ways languages influence each other, and the relation which their word-stocks bear to one another. As the Indo-Europeans migrated, they overpowered the natives of the lands which they entered; if they failed to conquer, they were themselves enslaved by their victors, and as Indo-Europeans they disappeared. For, be it noted and remembered, blood inheritance and

[10]

linguistic inheritance are two very different things : the fact that English is the language of a country, does not necessarily mean that the ancestors of its inhabitants fifteen centuries ago spoke Anglo-Saxon, though their speech ancestors must have done so. The best example on a large scale is seen in the full-blooded Negroes of the United States, none of whose blood ancestors even three centuries ago spoke a word of English. Thus in the migrations of the Indo-Europeans, those whom they conquered became their slaves, learned their language, and eventually were absorbed into the same stock ; some change in the speech of the conquerors was at the same time produced by the indigenous element. But their language remained essentially Indo-European, which enables us to make comparisons such as we have given ; the gaps indicate that Roumanian and Lithuanian use other words for *father*, not related to the usual word. The difficulties and problems produced by such substitutions may here be disregarded.

Where the inherited words have persisted, appearing in unchanged or somewhat altered form, the words of the different languages are said to be *cognate* to each other. English *father* and Latin *pater* are cognates ; that is, they are akin, descendants of a common linguistic ancestor in the direct line. Though they have changed certain of their sounds in the course of centuries, the philologist, by gathering the instances, can formulate the laws of these changes, even as the chemist gathers his phenomena and is then able to express in formulae the chemical changes which take place when certain substances are brought together under definite conditions.

But words may be related to each other not by *cognation*, but by *borrowing*. When North America was settled, the colonists met certain strange objects for which they had no terms of their own; and not unnaturally they often adopted, with alterations, the words used by the natives. Thus from various North American Indian languages, English has taken *hickory, hominy, moose, opossum, skunk, toboggan, tomahawk, wigwam*. Such words are known as *borrowed words* or *loan words*.

English *father* is a cognate of Latin *pater;* but English *paternal* is not a cognate of Latin *paternalis*, it is a borrowed form of it, as the initial *p* shows. *Stand* is a cognate of Latin *status; state* is the borrowed form of Latin *status*, and not a cognate. Oftentimes an old inherited word and a new borrowed word can be distinguished only by the difference in the sound changes, a difficult task requiring a mastery of the technical minutiae of the subject. From this we must here forbear; yet we must stress the point, that the debt of the English language to Greece and Rome consists of borrowings, and that the present study is therefore a study in borrowed words, which must be carefully sifted out from among the original stock.

We now proceed to a brief history of the three languages with whose relations we are concerned: the Greek, the Latin, the English, which belong to the Greek, the Italic, and the Teutonic branches, respectively, of the Indo-European family of languages.

III. THE GREEK LANGUAGE

AMONG the migrating bands of Indo-Europeans were those whose descendants we know in historic times as Greeks. Passing southward, they entered the Balkan peninsula and settled in its southern portion, subduing the previous inhabitants, who appear vaguely in Greek literature as Pelasgians. The Greeks spread further to the islands and shores of the Eastern Mediterranean, and, what is here more important, to Sicily and the shores of South Italy, which from the number of colonies and the extent of the land received the name *Magna Graecia* or Great Greece, as contrasted with the smaller country from which they came.

The colonies in Sicily and Italy were the channels through which Greek influence was first exerted on the Latin language. Established before Rome made herself a factor in history, they included, among many other places, Cumae, near Naples, founded about 800 B.C., which gave the alphabet to the nations of Italy; Syracuse in Sicily, founded 734, at one time the greatest of all Greek cities; and Tarentum, throughout ancient times one of the three chief cities of Italy, founded about 720.

Commerce was the impulse to this colonization; and in commercial relations, inevitably, the language of the trader impresses upon the less developed media of speech — less developed in their adequacy for commercial intercourse — many of its own words denoting ideas and wares which the others had formerly lacked and for which they therefore had no words. Thus the Greek settlers gave many words to the languages of Italy, especially to the Oscan with which in South Italy they came into closer contact; and from the Oscan certain of these passed into Latin as well. The greatest gift of this early colonization, however, was the alphabet, which we reserve for a separate chapter.

The later influence of Greece on Rome was produced by military and political conditions. The spread of Roman dominion through Italy in the fourth and third centuries brought the Romans into conflict with the Greeks, for the first time, notably, in the war with Tarentum and with Pyrrhus, King of Epirus; this was fought mainly in South Italy, 280–275, and culminated in the capture of Tarentum, in 272. As yet the Romans had no developed literature; but the capture of Tarentum marked a new era for them, if, as is probable, a youth named Andronicus was among the captives. Becoming teacher of his master's sons, Andronicus composed in the rough Italian measure called the Saturnian, a brief Latin version of the *Odyssey*, for use as a school-book; set free with the name of Titus Livius Andronicus, he in 240 translated or adapted into a Latin version a Greek tragedy and a Greek comedy, to be performed at a festival celebrating the successful conclusion of the First Punic War. Gnaeus Naevius, who lived about 269–199, probably came from Campania, where Greek influence was paramount, and likewise translated or adapted Greek plays; he composed also an epic poem in Saturnians, on the First Punic War, in which he had taken part. Quintus Ennius, 239–169, was a native of Rudiae in Calabria, and knew Greek as he did Latin; in addition to adapting Greek plays, he composed an epic on the history of Rome, the *Annales*, which we know by some passages quoted by other authors. In it he used not the native meter, but the Greek dactylic hexameter, to the demands of which Latin was not particularly well suited; but so strong was Greek influence that this measure was at once established as the sole vehicle for Latin epic and didactic poetry, until after the close of the classical period.

Thus these three early Latin writers, three of the first four important writers of Latin (the Umbrian T. Maccius Plautus is the fourth), were thorough Greeks in education and outlook, and mark the mastery of Greek influence over the Latin literature and language. Notably, the technical terminology of Latin in philosophy and natural science, in grammar and literary criticism, is either borrowed from Greek or literally translated. Latin in this way contains a great number of Greek words, even as English is permeated with Latin words.

These words did not come in all at one time, but through a period of many centuries. The final conquest of Greece by Rome was marked by the sack of Corinth in 146 B.C.; and at about the same time several Greek philosophers and grammarians found their way to Rome and introduced the formal study of their subjects. The presence in Rome of great numbers of slaves who were Greek either by birth or by language or by both, added to the Greek influence. The spread of Christianity in the early centuries of our era was another occasion for the introduction of Greek words, as technical terms of the new religion; some of these words had earlier been taken into Greek from Hebrew. In the fourth century, the Roman court had become so Hellenized that the seat of the Empire was transferred to Constantinople. Later, in the Middle Ages, Greek was forgotten in the western part of the Empire, except for Arabic versions of Greek authors brought by the Mohammedans in their conquests; these were again translated, into Latin. But when Constantinople was about to fall into the hands of the Mohammedans, as it did in 1453, many scholars withdrew from that city to Italy, carrying with them manuscripts of Greek authors; and the resulting rebirth of Greek studies in the West was a very important factor in the revival of learning called the Renaissance. Since that time, the Greek language has continuously influenced the modern languages; it is a never failing storehouse from which terms are constantly being drawn, to meet the needs of an age which, while making giant strides in all branches of science and of industry, yet lacks the words which may fitly convey the new ideas.

IV. THE LATIN LANGUAGE

EVEN as certain Indo-European bands reached the Balkan peninsula and became the Greeks, others moved gradually westward and southward into Italy. They may have been that strange people who dwelt in villages built upon the lakes of Germany, Switzerland, and North Italy, whom we term *Lake-Dwellers*. However that may be, at the opening of recorded history they were in Central Italy. They did not all speak precisely alike: Latin was the tongue only of Rome and of the immediate vicinity, and even the neighboring towns Tusculum and Praeneste had their marked peculiarities of speech. The dialect of Falerii, to the north, was quite different; and still more divergent dialects were spoken among the Umbrians, among the Sabines and Marsians and others in Central Italy, and among the Samnites and Campanians, whose language is called Oscan.

Latin was then, when we first meet it, the speech of but a small district. Even before it spread with the extension of Roman rule, it was subject to certain outside influences. Not far from 1000 B.C., an alien folk called the Etruscans had come across the seas from Asia Minor to the west coast of Italy, where they conquered the Umbrians north of the Tiber, penetrated into the Po valley, were for some time masters of Campania, and held sway over Rome itself for no mean period. They gave the Romans much of their divination and of their religious system, many of their building methods, a simple form of drama, and many family names. At this same period, the Latin was subject not only to the influence of the kindred dialects, Sabine, Oscan, and Umbrian, but must have been somewhat transformed by the absorption, into the Roman body politic, of those peoples who had been the aborigines in the district; these natives were probably the close kin of the Ligurians of Northwest Italy, who in part preserved their independence until the reign of Augustus. Greek influence also began early, and continued for many centuries, as we have already seen. In the Punic Wars of the third and second centuries B.C., the Romans came into contact with a Semitic people, and received certain words, doubtless, from them; they again came under Semitic influence from the Jews and from the Christians, from the latter chiefly through the medium of Greek. The incursions of the Gauls into Italy, culminating in the capture and sack of Rome in the early fourth century, left the Gauls in the possession of North Italy; they seem to have given the Romans some words, mostly relating to warfare and horsemanship.

Latin, despite these admixtures, did not become a heterogeneous language like English; the only identifiable element of great bulk is the Greek, and even that had not the extreme importance to Latin which the Latin element in English has to English. More like English in another respect, Latin spread from a tiny spot beside the Tiber until it covered all the lands around the Mediterranean and all of Western Europe, an unbelievable growth — did we not know its history. This result was produced in Italy by the successive defeat and subjection of the Etruscans, the Umbrians, the Samnites, the Greek cities of the South, the Gauls of the North, and finally of the Ligurians in the North-west. The First Punic War resulted in an extension of Roman power in Sicily, and in the interval between the First and the Second Punic

Wars the Romans seized Sardinia also. Corsica was won by the Romans in the First Punic War, though imperfectly subjugated until much later. The Second Punic War gave Rome a temporary check, but its close found the Roman power advanced in Spain and in Africa around Carthage, which became definitely Roman after the destruction of Carthage in 146. In the first half of the second century Rome acquired most of Greece and of Macedonia, and in the latter half conquered and made a province of southeastern France, which for this reason is still known as *Provence*. Another check to Roman progress, though a short one, came in 90–88, in the Social War, when the allies of Rome in Central and South-Central Italy set up a counter confederation with its capital at Corfinium and tried to displace Rome as leader of Italy, but in vain. The language of this Italic Confederacy was Oscan, as we know from the legends on its coins. After this, however, came the rapid extension of Roman dominion in Spain and in Asia Minor and Egypt by Pompey, in Gaul by Julius Caesar, and then in various parts of the East by Caesar after his victory over Pompey. At the end of Augustus' reign, the Roman Empire included all Europe west of the Rhine and

south of the Danube, except Britain and a part
of Moesia on the Danube; all North Africa
except Mauritania or Morocco; practically
all of Asia Minor and the lands bordering the
eastern end of the Mediterranean. Southern
Britain, the unconquered part of Moesia, and
Mauritania became provinces within thirty
years after Augustus' death, and northern
England about forty years later. Further conquests in Asia, however, were ephemeral, and
may be passed over; but the conquest of Dacia,
by Trajan, soon after 100 A.D., is of real significance, though Roman power vanished from
this land at about the end of the fourth century,
even as it did from Britain.

Into all these lands the Latin language advanced along with Roman military and political
power, becoming the official language and, in
some countries, the vernacular also; yet in many
sections the local language persisted for centuries. Punic, for example, was still spoken
about Carthage in the fourth century of the
Christian era, more than 500 years after that
city had been destroyed; Greek [3] more than
held its own in the Greek lands, and Aquitanian,
mentioned by Caesar as different from the language of the other Gauls, has persisted to this

day in the speech of the Basques of Southwest France and North Spain. In Asia, in Britain, and in North Africa, Latin finally disappeared. But Latin remained the vernacular of many countries, assuming new and different forms with the lapse of time. Italian, in many dialects, is spoken in Italy and in the large islands of the Mediterranean. French is the language of France, southern Belgium, and western Switzerland, as well as of the French colonies; but another development of Latin, the Provençal, is the vernacular of southern France. Spanish is the language of Spain, and has been transplanted to most of America south of the United States, and to other present and past Spanish colonies, notably to the Philippines. Portuguese is spoken in Portugal and in Brazil. Rhaetian is spoken in several valleys on the border of Switzerland, Austria, and Italy. Roumanian is the language of Roumania, and of some colonies in Macedonia; and the persistence of this Latin language in a land which was held by the Romans for only a short time, is a striking proof of the grip of Roman civilization.

All these languages, it should be noted, developed from the colloquial Latin. But the literary language also persisted in scholarly use; and although the speakers changed the pronunciation of certain sounds to keep pace with the local pronunciation of the vernacular, classical Latin is still used with comparatively slight alteration as the international language of the priesthood of the Roman Catholic Church. Latin has had also a mighty influence on other languages which are not primarily derived from it: English and German are full of Latin words, Albanian is overloaded with them, Greek, Lithuanian, Russian have many; practically every language of the civilized or semi-civilized world contains at least a few words of Latin ancestry, received directly from Latin or through the mediation of some other tongue.

V. THE ENGLISH LANGUAGE

THE speakers of English are first heard of not on the island of Britain, but on the mainland of Europe, along the coast of Denmark or western Germany. They spoke a Teutonic dialect, closest akin to the Frisian, and not very different from the so-called Old Saxon of northern Germany and from the older form of Dutch. They had already been reached by the Roman military power and by Roman traders, from whom they had taken a few words, such as, probably, *mint*,[4] from Latin *moneta*, and *port*, from Latin *portus*.[5]

In the fourth century, these continental tribes harassed Britain by piratical descents, adding to the troubles of the Romans in governing the island. Then, with the increasing invasions of barbarian tribes into southern Europe, the Romans withdrew their forces from Britain and abandoned it in the beginning of the fifth century. Not long after, the continental tribes whom we know as Angles, Saxons, and Jutes, entered the island, either by invitation of the

Britons as aid against northern enemies, or as refugees from powerful foes at home. With increasing numbers, they became masters of southern and eastern England (so-called from the Angles), driving out or enslaving the native Britons.

These Britons spoke a Celtic language which even to-day survives in the Welsh spoken in much of Wales; they had absorbed certain Latin words during more than three centuries of Roman rule. To their Anglo-Saxon masters they transmitted some genuine Celtic words, such as *down*, meaning 'hill,' which appears also in the adverbial phrase *adown*, shortened to the preposition *down*, and in town names such as *Lon-don*.[6] They gave over also some words which they had adapted from Latin, notably *street* from (*via*) *strata* [7] 'paved road'; *mile* from *milia* (*passuum*) 'thousands (of paces)'; *Chester* from *castra* 'camp,' appearing also as the final part of *Win-chester*, *Wor-cester*, *Lan-caster;* and, probably, *coln* in *Lin-coln*, from *colonia* 'colony.'

Other Latin words came into Anglo-Saxon, or Old English, with the missionary work of St. Augustine, who landed in Britain in 597. The language lacked most of the words necessary

[27]

to express the technical ideas of Christianity, and the gaps had to be filled by borrowings from Latin. Some of these Latin words had come into Latin from Greek, and a few had come into Greek from Semitic before they passed into Latin and thence into English. Among these words are *church, devil, minster, school, clerk, deacon, synod, stole, anthem, organ, pope, priest,* all taken from Greek into Latin before they passed into Anglo-Saxon; *abbot,* from a Semitic dialect (Syriac), and *angel,* from Persian, passing through Greek and Latin into Anglo-Saxon; *alb, cope, nun, shrine, mass, font, shrove* (in *Shrove Tuesday*) and *shrive,* which are from pure Latin, or at any rate not traceable beyond Latin. A few words of this period seem to have been taken first into Irish, and then brought by Irish missionaries to England: such are the words *Christ, alms, monk,* which start as Greek; *tunic,* which is originally Semitic; *ass, verse,*[8] *fiddle, fan* (for winnowing), *kiln,* which cannot be traced beyond Latin.[9] These words are recognized as having passed through Irish, by some peculiar development in the sounds, as for example the long vowel in the name *Christ,* and the *f* in *fan* for the *v* of Latin *vannus.*

Not long before 800, the Scandinavians from

Denmark or Norway began their raids on eastern England north of the Thames. Soon they took to building fortified camps on the shore, even passing the winter there; and in the time of Alfred the Great (871–900), they were masters of all England lying north of a line from Chester to London. In the early eleventh century, the Danish Canute became by force of arms the acknowledged ruler of all England. Through this Scandinavian element, the English language received a great number of words, which are the harder to identify because many words were almost or quite identical in the two tongues. Some we know by an *sc* or *sk* which has remained, instead of changing to *sh* as in Anglo-Saxon: *scalp*, *score*, *skill*, *sky*. Others have a *g* not changed to *j* or *y* in sound: *gate*, *give*, *get*, *guest*. Some keep *k* unchanged, as in *ken*, *keel*, *kid*, *kilt*, *kink*. Still others are *earl*, *dwell*, *law*, *take*, *wrong;* even the common pronouns *them*, *they*, *their* and the adverbs *fro* and *though* show Scandinavian peculiarities. By such means we recognize a few words which came from Latin into English by way of the Scandinavian: *kettle*, from Latin *catillus* 'bowl'; *kirtle*, from *curtus* 'shortened,' but with an added suffix; *skirt*, from an inferred Latin *excurtus*,

[29]

equivalent to *curtus* (pure Anglo-Saxon borrowings are seen in *short* and *shirt*); and perhaps *kindle*, from Latin *candela* 'candle.'[10]

Edward the Confessor, King of England from
1042 to 1066, had spent many years in exile
at the Norman court on the continent, and upon
succeeding to the English throne was a center
of Norman-French influence. This must have
affected the language of the island; but the
great French influence dates from 1066, when,
after the death of Edward, the Saxon King
Harold was defeated and slain at Hastings by
the invading Duke of Normandy, William,
known as the Conqueror. For some centuries
after this, the language of the court and of polite
society was French; at first, the dialect of Normandy, but later, after the Angevin line came
to the throne in 1154, the central French, of
which the literary French of to-day is the modern representative. The difference appears in
such words as *catch* and *chase*, the former coming
from Norman-French and the latter from central French, but both going back to one Latin
original; it is seen also in *warden* and *guardian*,
both being derivatives of one root borrowed from
a Germanic dialect, but with diverse initial
sounds because they are drawn from the two

French dialects. There is no evidence that during the use of French in the court and in polite society the Anglo-Saxon language was put under prohibition or disabilities; but its lowering in the social scale accounts for its decline, and for its failure to retain or to develop the phraseology of polite intercourse, of learning, and of the arts and professions. One of the Anglo-Saxon *Chronicles* was indeed continued to the year 1154, but with its close the Anglo-Saxon literature was ended. Yet the Anglo-Saxon language, or as we must now speak of it, the English language, remained the tongue of the great mass of the people, and in 1362 the English speech was required in the courts of law on the ground that French was not generally understood. Henry IV, born in 1367, spoke English as his mother tongue, though he was the first of English rulers to do so since 1066. At about this same time, private documents composed in English begin to appear, though sparingly; legal proclamations continue to be in Latin or in French or in both, to the exclusion of English, until 1488. Yet the decline of French even in the polite classes is indicated by a statute of the University of Oxford, probably of the thirteenth century, which enjoins instruction both in English and in French, "that the French language be not entirely left out"; this may indicate that the French of England had deteriorated from the continental standard, but certainly shows that English had come again into its own. Several statutes of colleges at Oxford between 1332 and 1340 require students to use Latin and French exclusively, evidently from a fear that they would be lost as spoken languages under the encroachment of English. In 1385 all children learned English rather than French in the so-called "Latin schools." Chaucer, the first preëminent writer who used the English speech as modified by the Norman-French influence, died in 1400.

Before proceeding, we must digress for a clearer understanding of the speech which was introduced into England by the Norman Conquest. The piratical Northmen who raided and finally conquered England had not spared the neighboring shores of the continent; they harried especially the lower valley of the Seine, repeatedly occupying Rouen. In 911, the French king Charles the Simple ceded to Rolf or Rollo, the chief of the Northmen, a district of which Rouen was the capital. These Northmen spoke Danish, a Scandinavian dialect of the Teutonic group, even as did the Norse invaders of England; but in their new home, although Danish was still spoken along the coasts as late as the twelfth century, they adopted in general the local French dialect, into which they carried only a few of their Teutonic words. Their name was softened from Northmen to Normans, and the district was called Normandy. The French speech which they assumed, was chiefly Latin, but not exclusively so; for it contained many words taken from the Gallic dialects spoken there before the Roman conquest by Julius Caesar. There was also an infusion of Teutonic words from the migrating German tribes who had been moving westward into that region for many centuries.

The Norman-French language which the Norman conquest introduced into England, was therefore a language mainly Latin with the normal borrowings of older date, especially from Greek, but with the addition of some Gallic words (*i.e.*, Celtic), some Teutonic words of the earlier invasions, and some Teutonic words from the Normans themselves. The central French differed, in lacking the words which the Normans brought to France, as well as in having different pronunciations for certain sounds. But an extremely high percentage of both dialects, we must emphasize, consisted of pure Latin words, modified in sound and in spelling, and not infrequently in meaning. As a result of this, we find, on opening the works of Chaucer, that the classical element [11] has enormously improved its position in English. In the prologue of the *Canterbury Tales*, only one of every four verses in the first two hundred lines lacks a word of classical origin; and in every hundred verses of the prologue, there are somewhat over one hundred classical words. One hundred verses contain between 750 and 800 words; the classical words amount therefore to about fifteen percent.

The period of the Tudor sovereigns (1485–1603) was also the period of the Renaissance, and another great influx of classical words took place. Some came in unchanged forms, precisely as they appear in Latin or in Greek; others underwent slight changes. Still others came from French and from Italian, in the forms which they had in those languages; these were chiefly words which had to do with polite society and with the arts and literature. Others came from Spanish and from Portuguese, because of contact between the navigators of the nations in that era of exploration and development of trade-routes: among such words which are of Latin origin, are *negro*, *cargo*, *armadillo*, and *alligator*, from Spanish words, and *caste*, *cobra*, and *moidore*, from Portuguese words. A considerable accession of Dutch words, brought about by the same factors, betrays little or no Latin influence; these words have to do almost exclusively with shipping and with trade. The close of the period may be typified by the works of Shakespeare (1564–1616) and the appearance of the Authorized or King James Version of the Bible in 1611.

During the seventeenth century, the process of adding to the English vocabulary continued, mainly from sources which are Latin or Greek, directly or indirectly. In fact, any Latin word might at that time be taken over, with only a suitable modification of the ending, or addition of a Latin prefix or suffix, and used freely in English; every Latin word was then potentially an English word. But about the time when William and Mary replaced the Stuart line on the throne, in 1689, there was a settling in the language which resulted in the disappearance of many words which had failed to prove their

[35]

utility. The words which survived, however, have with few exceptions remained in use down to the present day.

The final great addition of Latin and Greek words has come with the epoch of mechanical inventions, and the development of the sciences along lines and into fields which hitherto had hardly been foreshadowed even in the vaguest way. To illustrate, it suffices to mention the steam-engine, electricity, the telegraph and the telephone, the automobile and the aëroplane, radium and radio-activity. New words based on Greek and Latin are appearing almost daily to denote new scientific ideas or instruments or machines, and to denote new articles of trade. The advertising columns of the periodicals are rich in such words.

But before turning to some selected lists and examples, we may record the extension of the English language geographically. In about the year 1600, English was spoken only in the is-land of Britain, where it had as rivals Gaelic in Scotland, Welsh in Wales, and Cornish in Cornwall; not to mention the use of Latin as the language of scholars and, until shortly be-fore, that of French as the language of aristo-cratic society. Before that date, the only notable use of English in other lands was in an English colony in southeastern Ireland, in the county of Wexford, where an English settlement had maintained its language since its foundation in 1169. But in the last three centuries, English has spread to all the lands which are or have been subject to the British crown, where it thrives in an amicable competition with native languages : we may name Canada, India, Australia, New Zealand, Egypt, the Union of South Africa, and the innumerable smaller colonies and protectorates on continents and islands, and our own United States of America, from which English is spreading into Porto Rico, the Philippines, Hawaii, the Panama Canal Zone, and some smaller localities. As the language of the greatest commercial nations which the world has ever seen, English has been used as a medium of trade in many other lands, also, and has even become the main element in that peculiar language used in Chinese countries and known as Pidgin English. As a medium of learning, English has extensive use in Japan, and it is used in China in colleges, at the express desire of the Chinese students. All in all, English bade fair to become by natural selection the world language for general international use, when the Great War came and left national animosities which will indefinitely prevent such employment of any one modern national language. The factor of most importance in bringing English to its present wide employment has been the great commercial activity of its speakers; but a very important contributory factor has been the presence, in it, of a tremendous number of words which in the same or closely similar form appear also in most or all of the other developed languages of civilization. These words are almost without exception of Greek or Latin stock.

We may now give a few illustrations of the extent to which at different periods the English language has been permeated with words derived or borrowed from the classical languages.

VI. STATISTICS AND EXAMPLES

WE have seen the paths by which classical words entered English; we must now examine the actual proportion of such words in English at different times.

Let us start with the Anglo-Saxon poem known as *Beowulf;* this is essentially the oldest monument of English, though it has a few Christian accretions. The poem contains 3,182 verses, with about 17,500 words; the vocabulary contains slightly under 4,000 entries. Of these, there are 39 words which are in part or wholly taken from Latin; they occur a total of 92 times. In other terms, one percent of the vocabulary and one half of one percent of total words used, are of classical origin. If we include 11 other words, with 30 occurrences, of possible but not certain Latin origin, the percentages are raised a trifle. The 39 certain words come from 17 Latin words, as follows: *camp* 'battle,' *cempa* 'warrior' (cf. *champion*), from *campus* 'field'; *candel*, from *candela; ceaster* 'camp' (cf. *Chester*), from *castra; gimm* 'gem,' from *gemma;*

[39]

myntan 'to intend,' from *moneta* 'mint, coin' (cf. *mint*); *nōn* 'noon,' from *nona* (*hora*) 'ninth hour, 3 P.M.'; *scrīfan* 'to mete out' (cf. *shrive*), from *scribere* 'to write'; *strǣt* 'street,' from (*via*) *strata* 'paved (street)'; *orc* 'pitcher,' from *urceus;* *weall* 'wall,' from *vallum;* *wīc* 'village,' (cf. *Ber-wick, Green-wich*), from *vicus;* *wīn* 'wine,' from *vinum;* *ancor,* from *ancora;* *dēofol* 'devil,' from *diabolus;* *disc* 'dish,' from *discus;* *draca* 'dragon,' from *draco;* *gīgant* 'giant,' from *gigas.* The last five had come into Latin from Greek.

To take another example from Anglo-Saxon, the *Elene* of Cynewulf, who lived about the year 800, contains 1,320 verses, with about 7,000 words and about 2,000 entries in the vocabulary. The classical element includes 46 vocabulary entries, occurring 117 times, and coming from 32 Latin words.[12] This makes 2.3 percent of the vocabulary entries and 1.7 percent of the total number of words, a considerable increase over the figures for *Beowulf;* but the increase is largely in words which have to do with the Christian religion and with the government of the Roman empire, for the *Elene* has as subject the discovery of the true cross by the empress Helena.

In the entire vocabulary of Anglo-Saxon, that
is, of English down to about 1150, we can identify between 450 and 500 Latin and Greek words,
borrowed with or without change. Of these,
over 150 came into Latin from Greek; and a
considerable number came from Hebrew or
some other Semitic dialect into Latin either
directly or through Greek. Some appear not
in classical Latin, but only in late Latin, coming
from Celtic or from Germanic or from a source
not determinable. Now, of the entire Anglo-
Saxon vocabulary, almost three fourths has
disappeared, leaving no representatives in modern English; but the words taken from Latin
had a much greater vitality, and nearly all of
them are still in use, although many have had
an interrupted history — that is, the old forms
have been remade so as to look more like the
original Latin. The following lists of such
words are for intelligibility given in the modern
forms; it must be remembered that some have
changed their meanings since Anglo-Saxon
days. Arranged by groups, they illustrate the
wide range of Anglo-Saxon use of Latin materials. The words of the first group denote ideas
concerned with the church and with religion;
over half of these came into Latin from Greek:

abbess	*chaplain*	*disciple*	*prime*
abbot	*chapter*	*epistle*	*provost*
acolyte	*choir*	*font*	*psalm*
alb	*chrism*	*grade*	*psalter*
alms	*chrisom*	*hymn*	*pure*
altar	*Christ*	*idol*	*purple*
anchorite	*Christian*	*martyr*	*relic*
angel	*church*	*mass*	*response*
anti-Christ	*cither*	*master*	*rule*
anthem	*cleric*	*minster*	*saint*
apostate	*cloister*	*monk*	*shrift*
apostle	*close*	*noon*	*shrine*
arch-bishop	*cope*	*nun*	*shrive*
arch-deacon	*cowl*	*offer*	*stole*
Arian	*creed*	*offering*	*synod*
ark	*crown*	*organ*	*taper*
bishop	*crutch*	*pall*	*temple*
camel	*crypt*	*Pharisee*	*title*
candle	*cup*	*pope*	*tract*
canon	*cymbal*	*porch*	*tribute*
canticle	*dalmatic*	*preach*	*trope-(book)*
cell	*deacon*	*preacher*	
chalice	*devil*	*priest*	

Education, of which the church was the agent, shows the following classical words:

accent	*grammar*	*paper*	*scholar*
to decline	*meter*	*school*	*verse*

[42]

As the church was the agent also of medicine and of pharmaceutics, we find many plant names taken from classical sources, with which, for convenience, we include names of other plants and fruits:

aloe	cummin	lovage	periwinkle
balsam	cypress	mallow	pimpernel
beet	dragon(wort)	millet	plant
betony	elm	mint	plum
cedar	fennel	myrrh	poppy
celandine	feverfew	(tur)nip	radish
centaury	fig	onion	rose
cherry	flower(y)	palm	rue
chervil	ginger	panic	rush
chest(nut)	hyssop	parsley	sage
cod-(apple)	jacinth	pea	savine
coriander	laurel	peach	savory
cornel	lentil	pear	spelt
cost(mary)	lettuce	pellitory	spike(nard)
cress	lily	pepper	vervain

The elements in parentheses in these lists were lacking either in Latin or in Anglo-Saxon, in the combinations here given. We may next list names of animals:

ass	lamprey	ostrich	trout
capon	lion	oyster	turtle-(dove)

dolphin	*lobster*	*pea(cock)*
dragon	*mule*	*phoenix*
elephant	*mussel*	*tiger*

There is also a group of words connected with government, warfare, and the like:

arbalest	*chancellor*	*mile*	*street*
Caesar	*Chester*	*military*	*wall*
camp	*cohort*	*notary*	*-wick*
champion	*consul*	*palace*	
castle	*league*	*pike*	

Then there is a larger group of words connected with the ordinary life of the household:

amphora	*flask*	*oil*	*soap*
belt	*fork*	*pillow*	*sock*
box	*kettle*	*pin*	*sole*
butter	*kitchen*	*plaster*	*spend*
cheese	*linen*	*plate*	*sponge*
chest	*mantle*	*pound*	*stove*
cook	*mat*	*purse*	*table*
dish	*mortar*	*sack*	*tunic*
fan	*must*	*skirt*	*wine*

The remaining words may be thrown into one miscellaneous group:

adamant	*date*	*mount*	*scrofula*
alum	*double*	*orchard*	*seal*

anchor	*fever*	*part*	*secure*
April	*fiddle*	*pigment*	*short*
bastard	*fuller*	*to pine*	*sign*
bezant	*gem*	*pipe*	*sound*
bin	*giant*	*pit*	*spade*
calends	*inch*	*pitch*	*spelter*
callow	*kiln*	*place*	*story*
chalk	*lake*	*plume*	*strop*
circle	*line*	*pole*	*to temper*
colter	*marble*	*port*	*term*
column	*market*	*to prove*	*tile*
copper	*mechanical*	*pumice*	*timbrel*
cordwainer	*mill*	*punt*	*tower*
crisp	*to mint*	*to rage*	*to turn*
crystal	*to mix*	*Satur(day)*	*tragic*

There are other words which Anglo-Saxon adopted from Latin; but either they left no descendants in modern English, or they do not lend themselves so well to representation in their modern forms. The grouping which we have made is rough, and open to improvement; yet these lists illustrate fairly well the extent to which Anglo-Saxon, or English before 1150 A.D., borrowed from the Latin language, and through Latin from the Greek.

There is a difference, however, in the degree

to which these words made themselves at home in their new environment. Some were borrowed without change, and always acted as strangers; others were treated like native words in derivation and word formation. For example, from Latin *campus* 'field,' we find not merely *camp* 'battle,' but the compounds *camp-gimm* 'precious stone' (*gimm* from Latin *gemma*), *un-camp-rōf* 'unwarlike' (Anglo-Saxon *rōf* 'strong'), *woruld-camp* 'secular warfare,' *ge-camp* 'warfare,' and 11 other compounds; *camp-ian* 'to fight,' *camp-ung* 'the act of fighting,' *ge-camp-ian* 'to gain by fighting'; the derivative *cempa* 'soldier,' *efen-cempa* 'fellow-soldier,' and 3 other compounds; *cempestre* 'female novice.' Latin *Christus*, which is from Greek, yields Anglo-Saxon *Crīst* 'Christ,' *crīst-lic* 'Christian,' *crīst-mæsse* 'Christmas' (*mæsse* from Latin *missa*), *crīst-en* 'Christian,' *crīsten-dōm* and *crīsten-nes* or *crīst-nes* 'Christianity,' *crīsten-ian* 'to christen,' *crīsten-ung* 'christening,' *efen-crīsten* 'fellow-Christian,' *un-crīsten* 'infidel.'

We see from these that the borrowed Latin words were used freely in the formation of compounds; naturally, they were inflected like native words, except in rare instances where substantives kept some Latin endings or were indeclinable. There was a free use of native suffixes, as in the examples just given, and in *mynet-ere* 'money-changer, minter,' from *mynet* 'coin,' Latin *moneta*; *tigel-en* 'of earthenware,' from *tigele* 'tile,' Latin *tegula*; *Iūdē-isc* 'Jewish,' from *Iūdēas* 'Jews,' Latin *Iudaei*; *un-ge-segn-od* 'not marked with the sign of the cross,' from *segn-ian* 'to sign,' *segn* 'sign,' Latin *signum*; *apostel-hād* 'apostlehood,' from *apostel*, Latin *apostolus*. Other suffixes than those here given are of less frequent occurrence joined to Latin borrowings; and of the prefixes, though a number are so used, the only usual ones are the negative *un* and the participial *ge*, both already exemplified. To return to actual compounds, there are at least 135 Latin words which were used in Anglo-Saxon as the prior element of compounds, and at least 66 which were used as the second element. Occasionally a Latin compound was translated part by part into Anglo-Saxon, as when *pro-scriptio* became *fore-writen-nes*, and *quinque-folium* 'cinquefoil' became *fīf-lēaf*.

It is after the Norman conquest that the great influx of Latin words into English takes place. It was noted above that the classical words in Chaucer's *Canterbury Tales* amount to 15 percent of the total number. The following extract (*Prologue*, 477–490) is from the description of the "poor parson"; the words coming from Latin are put in italics, and those from Greek in capitals:

A good man was ther of *religioun*,
And was a *poure Persoun* of a toun;
But riche he was of holy thoght and werk.
He was also a lerned man, a *CLERK*,
That *CRIST*es gospel trewely wolde *preche;*
His *PARISSH*ens *devout*ly wolde he teche,
Benigne he was, and wonder *diligent*,
And in *adversitee* ful *pacient;*
And swich he was y-*preved* ofte sythes.
Ful looth were him to cursen for his tythes,
But rather wolde he yeven, out of *doute*,
Unto his *poure PARISSH*ens aboute
Of his *offr*ing, and eek of his *substaunce*.
He coude in litel thing han *suffisaunce*."

The typography shows that some of these classical words have taken on English prefixes and suffixes; among many other examples found in Chaucer are the following: bi*seged* 'besieged,' for*pyne*d 'exhausted with suffering' (*poena*), mis*governaunce*, mis*use*th, un*certain*,

[48]

un*couple*, un*discreet*, un*occupie*d, y-*punisshe*d; *cloister*er 'cloister-monk,' *forst*er 'forester,' *fyn*est 'finest,' *anoy*ful 'annoying,' *roll*inge 'rolling,' *dette*lees 'debtless,' *doute*less 'doubtless,' *rude*liche 'rudely,' *sodeyn*ly 'suddenly,' *solempne*ly 'solemnly,' *siker*ness 'sureness'; and the compounds *boter*-flye 'butterfly,' bremble-*flour* 'bramble-flower,' *countre*wayte 'counterweight,' *messe*-dayes 'mass-days,' *pea*cock, *Strat*ford.

We now pass to Shakespeare (1564–1616). Hamlet's soliloquy (*Hamlet*, III, 1) contains 255 words, of which 48 are classical, or 19 percent. The Seven Ages of Man (*As You Like It*, II, 7) contains 214 words, of which 54 are classical, or 25 percent. Portia's speech on "the quality of mercy" (*Merchant of Venice*, IV, 1) has 173 words, of which 40 are classical, or 23 percent. The appeal of Queen Katharine (*King Henry VIII*, II, 4) has 366 words, of which 69 are classical, or 19 percent. The average of these is 21 percent, which is about the average for Shakespeare in general.

But this is the figure per hundred words used, not per hundred *different* words used. If repetitions be omitted, the four passages have respectively 32, 33, 29, 33 percent of classical words. If they be grouped together and all duplications

[49]

eliminated, the percentage of classical words
rises to 40, since the words most repeated —
pronouns, articles, prepositions and conjunctions, the verbs *be* and *have* — are practically
all of Anglo-Saxon origin. One suspects, then,
that examination of the complete vocabulary of
Shakespeare will show a still higher percentage
of classical words.

We take a word concordance, and group the
words by their origins. With the Anglo-Saxon
words we place the words which have come into
English from the Celtic, from the Scandinavian,
from Dutch, and from German, either directly
or through French; with the classical words we
place those words which appear for the first
time in late Latin or in French, without indication of their remoter origin. We must not count
separately genitive and plural forms of nouns,
and personal and tense forms of verbs. This
done, we find that Shakespeare used 2501 words
beginning with A, B, and C, and that of these
there were 886 of Anglo-Saxon origin, or 35.5
percent, and 1615 of classical origin, or 65.5
percent. Let us try another method, eliminating obvious derivatives and compounds, except
those formed by prefixes: then there are 416
words beginning with D, including 130 of the

Anglo-Saxon group, or 32 percent, and 286 of the classical group, or 68 percent.

As for the Greek words in English at this time, direct importations must as yet have been few, but many had come through Latin. The English words coming from Greek, which begin with D and were used by Shakespeare, are the following; any prefixes of Latin origin are marked off by a hyphen: *d-affodil*, from ἀσφοδελός a kind of lily; *Dardan*, from Δαρδάνιος; *dauphin* and *dolphin*, from δελφῖν- 'dolphin'; *demon*, from δαίμων 'deity'; *de-pose* and *dis-pose*, from παῦσις 'pause'; *desk* and *dish*, from δίσκος 'round disc'; *devil*, from διάβολος 'slanderer'; *diadem*, from διάδημα 'band'; *dialect*, from διάλεκτος 'speech'; *dialogue*, from διάλογος; *diameter*, from διάμετρος; *diamond*, from ἀδάμας 'unconquerable'; *diaper*, from δίασπρος 'pure white'; *diet*, from δίαιτα 'mode of life'; *dilemma*, from δίλημμα 'double proposition'; *dis-burse* and *dis-pursed*, from βύρσα 'hide, leather'; *dis-card*, from χάρτης 'leaf of paper'; *dis-place*, from πλατεῖα 'broad (street)'; *di-sponge*, from σπόγγος 'sponge'; *drachma* and *dram*, from δραχμή a weight and coin; *dragon*, from δράκων; *dropsy*, from ὕδρωψ; *duell-ist*, from -ιστης suffix denoting

[51]

the agent. The number of Greek words with
this initial, appearing in Shakespeare's works,
though not very great, shows them to be an
element of importance.

Thus, to sum up, the classical words in Shakespeare appear to form approximately two
thirds of his vocabulary and one fifth of all
words used. Jaques' homily on the Seven
Ages of Man may serve as an illustration, with
the same indication of Latin and Greek words
as before :

All the world's a *stage*,
And all the men and women *mere*ly players :
They have their *exit*s and their *entrance*s ;
And one man in his time plays many *part*s,
His *act*s being seven *age*s. At first the *infant*,
Mewling and puking in the *nurse*'s arms.
And then the whining *SCHOOL*-boy, with his
SATCHel,
And shining morning *face*, creeping like snail
Unwillingly to *SCHOOL*. And then the lover,
Sighing like *furnace*, with a woful *ballad*
Made to his *mistrESS*' eye-brow. Then a *sol-
dier*,
Full of *strange* oaths, and bearded like the *PARD*,
JEALous in *honour*, *sudden* and quick in *quar-
rel*,
Seeking the bubble *reputation*

Even in the *CANNON*'s mouth.   And then the
  justice,
In fair *round* belly with good *CAPON* lin'd,
With eyes *severe*, and beard of *formal* cut,
Full of wise saws and *modern instance*s;
And so he plays his *part*.   The sixth *age* shifts
Into the lean and slipper'd *PANTALOON*,
With *spectacle*s on nose, and pouch on side;
His youthful hose, well *sav'd*, a world too wide
For his shrunk shank; and his big manly *voice*,
*Turn*ing again toward childish *treble*, *pipe*s
And whistles in his *sound*.   Last *SCENE* of all,
That ends this *strange event*ful *HISTORY*,
Is *second* childishness, and *mere oblivion*, —
Sans teeth, *sans* eyes, *sans* taste, *sans* everything.

The King James translation of the Bible was
made for the less educated classes, and, based
as it was on earlier English versions, often fails
to employ the words of classical origin, or even
avoids them; the educated classes knew Latin
and used the Bible in that language.   This
translation, therefore, contains fewer classical
words than do the plays of Shakespeare; yet
the sixth chapter of the *First Epistle to Timothy*,
with about 440 words, shows 19 percent of classical words.   But the subject matter is here
responsible for an abnormally large amount,
and the second chapter of the *Gospel according*

[53]

to St. Luke, with over 1000 words, is more nearly typical; it has but 11 percent of words of classical origin. Yet this should not mislead us: let us eliminate the much repeated words — articles, pronouns, prepositions and conjunctions, the verbs *be* and *have* and other auxiliaries, and the negative adverb. The remainder includes the words that carry the meaning, the excluded words being merely the props on which the important ideas are sustained; of this important remainder, at least 33 percent comes from the classical languages. For the meaning of the passage, then, the 11 percent of classical derivatives has a function far greater than that indicated by the percentage.

On the other hand, the writings of John Milton (1608-1674) might be suspected of containing an abnormally high percentage of classical words. Yet this is not everywhere so: *Il Penseroso*, with about 1050 words, has only 19 percent. But *Paradise Lost*, in its first 1000 words, shows over 25 percent, and the following specimen (I, 43-53) has 36 percent:

> Him the Almighty *Power*
> Hurled headlong *flam*ing from the *ETHEReal* sky,
> With *hideous ruin* and *combustion*, down
> To bottomless *perdition*, there to dwell

In *ADAMANTINE chains* and *PENal* fire,
Who durst *defy* the *Omnipotent* to *arm*s.
Nine times the *SPACE* that *measure*s day and night
To *mortal* men, he with his *horrid crew*,
Lay *vanquish*ed, *roll*ing in the fiery *GULF*,
*Confound*ed, though *immortal*.

A more recent poet, Alfred Tennyson (1809–1892), used in his non-dramatic poems about 2400 words beginning with A, B, and C; of these, 56 percent were derived from Latin and Greek, a considerably lower percentage than in Shakespeare; he is said to have taken pride in the purity of his English vocabulary. In percentage of all words used, the *Idylls of the King* (500 words each from the beginning of *The Coming of Arthur*, the beginning of *Merlin and Vivien*, and the end of *The Last Tournament*) give 10 percent of classical words; *In Memoriam* (1000 words at the beginning of Canto XX) gives 13 percent; *The Princess* (1000 words of the prologue) gives 17 percent. As the different works are quite uniform in themselves, giving a figure which additional compilation after 500 words does not change more than one percent, the variation among the works seems due to differences in the subject matter.

Robert Browning (1812–1889), in the first 1000 words of *Sordello*, uses 20 percent of classical words. Henry Wadsworth Longfellow (1807–1882) has 18 percent in the opening of the *Courtship of Miles Standish*, and only 15 percent in the canto of *Hiawatha* which is entitled *The Peace-Pipe*. Among poets still living, Alfred Noyes, in his *Drake* (the first 1000 words of Book I), has slightly under 18 percent of classical words. But technical writing contains a much higher percentage of such words. Examination of selected paragraphs in the last edition of the *Encyclopaedia Britannica*, from the articles on *Algebra*, *Alloys*, *Alps*, *Amphioxus* (two selections), and *Amphitheatre*, yielded respectively 40, 33, 31, 34, 40, and 39 percent of words derived from Latin and Greek.

We may sum up the results of our investigation in a few sentences. A considerable number of words came into Anglo-Saxon from Latin, some of them being Latinized Greek words; but they formed a very small part of the total vocabulary and of the total words used, although certain very familiar words were among them. Between the Norman Conquest and the time of Shakespeare so many words of classical origin were adopted by English, that the language had, in the time of the great dramatist, reached practically its present character; for Shakespeare's vocabulary showed about 65 percent of classical derivatives, and the present-day vocabulary of nearly 20,000 words, described in our first chapter, showed about 60 percent. In total words used, we find that poets of the last hundred years vary between 10 and 20 percent of classical words, which averages less than the percentage used by Shakespeare and by Milton. Recent technical writing runs at least as high as 40 percent. Other writing lies between these extremes. To test this formulation, the writer examined two editorials in his regular daily newspaper, and found that they contained respectively 26 and 29 percent of words derived from Greek and Latin. As they were chosen quite at random, except that they were both from the same day's issue and of considerable length, they give unbiased confirmation of the conclusion already reached.

VII. OUR PRESENT–DAY
VOCABULARY

L ET us consider now the stock of words in
use to-day, dividing it into the classical
and the Anglo-Saxon; perhaps the latter
should rather be called the non-classical, for
in evaluating the Latin and Greek influence on
English all words which do not come from the
classical languages directly or indirectly must
be thrown into the other group, which therefore
contains many words not Anglo-Saxon in origin.
But of the many ways in which our vocabulary
might be discussed, we must limit ourselves to a
few, especially the sources of our monosyllabic
words; classical and Anglo-Saxon synonyms;
the derivation of two or more English words
from one and the same classical word; and the
use of classical derivatives in special fields of
ordinary life and of science.

We start with the matter of monosyllables,
for there is a prevalent belief that monosyllables
are of native origin. But of the monosyllables
beginning with A, F, and R, 30 percent come

from the classical languages; of those beginning
with CA, we find, after eliminating the very
rare words, 25 classical words and only 15 non-
classical words. The latter are *calf*, *call*, *can*
'be able,' *can* 'receptacle,' *care*, *cart*, *caw*, from
Anglo-Saxon; *cake*, from Anglo-Saxon or Scandinavian; *carp* 'to disparage,' *cast*, from Scandinavian; *cam*, from Dutch; *carp* 'a fish,' *caul*,
from French; *cark*, from Celtic through French;
cat, probably from Celtic. The 25 words of
classical origin are the following, with the Latin
or Greek words from which they come: [13] *cab*,
from *caper* 'goat'; *cad*, from *capitellum* 'little
head'; *cage*, from *cavea* 'a hollow, stall'; *calm*,
from καῦμα 'heat'; *camp*, from *campus* 'plain';
cane, from κάννα 'reed'; *cant* 'talk,' from
cantare 'to sing'; *cant* 'edge, to tilt,' from
κάνθος 'corner of the eye, felloe of a wheel';
cap, from late Latin *cappa* 'cap'; *cape* 'gar-
ment,' from late Latin *capa* 'cape'; *cape* 'head-
land,' from *caput* 'head'; *car*, from *carrus*
'car'; *card* of pasteboard, from χάρτης 'leaf
of paper'; *card* for combing wool, from *carduus*
'thistle'; *case* in grammar, from *casus* 'falling';
case for books, and *cash*, from *capsa* 'box';
cask and *casque*, from *quassare* 'to burst';
caste, from *castus* 'pure'; *catch*, from *captare* 'to

[59]

seize'; *caulk*, from *calcare* 'to tread'; *cause*, from *causa* 'cause'; *cave*, from *cavus* 'hollow.' Thus brevity in a word is no sure sign of native English origin. The most striking example of the contrary is *alms*, which goes back through Anglo-Saxon and Latin to Greek, where the original was six-syllabled ἐλεημοσύνη 'pity.'

The double nature of our vocabulary is clearly seen in those instances where two words, one of classical origin and the other of native origin, are used side by side with little or no difference in meaning. The following are examples, the classical word being given first:

CLASSICAL	NATIVE	CLASSICAL	NATIVE
amicable	friendly	felicity	happiness
benediction	blessing	flour	meal
candor	openness	flower	bloom
carnal	fleshly	gentle	mild
close	shut	identity	sameness
commence	begin	illegality	unlawfulness
cordial	hearty	labor	work
deity	godhead	member	limb
desire	wish	multiple	manifold
double	twofold	novel	new
error	mistake	pastor	shepherd
paternal	fatherly	soiled	dirty
probability	likelihood	story	tale
purchase	buy	terror	dread

sentiment	*feeling*	*verity*	*truth*
sign	*token*	*virginity*	*maidenhood*

Such pairs are called *doublets;* but there are doublets also of another kind, which originate when one Latin or Greek word gives us two or even more English words, often of quite different meanings. One of the English words is usually taken directly from the Latin or Greek, with few if any changes; such words, because first borrowed by educated persons, are known as *learned words* or *book words*. The other word of the English pair has usually passed through French, in popular use through most or all of its history, so that it has undergone changes which very much obscure its origin. Thus *fragile* was taken direct from Latin *fragilis*, while *frail* underwent changes in French. But other influences also operate in producing such doublets: Latin *armata* 'armed' gives us *army* through the French and *armada* through the Spanish. Greek παραβολή became *parabola* in Latin, and this has given us *parabola* unchanged, and also *parable* through the old French, *parole* through the later French, and *palaver* from the Spanish *palabra* or the Portuguese *palavra* 'word.' Here are some further examples:

LATIN OR GREEK	DIRECT BORROWING			LESS DIRECT BORROWING
captivus	captive			caitiff
cohors	cohort			court
corona	corona			crown
factio	faction			fashion
gentilis	gentile	genteel		gentle
humanus	humane			human
invidiosus	invidious			envious
legalis	legal	leal		loyal
major	major			mayor
pallidus	pallid			pale
pendens	pendent			pendant
pietas	piety			pity
potio	potion			poison
quietus	quietus	quiet		coy
ratio	ratio	ration		reason
redemptio	redemption			ransom
rotundus	rotund			round
senior	senior	sire		sir
species	species	specie		spice
traditio	tradition			treason
vocalis	vocal			vowel
δίσκος	discus	disc	dish	desk
καμάρα	camera			chamber
πάπυρος	papyrus	paper		taper
παράλυσις	paralysis			palsy
πλατεῖα	place	piazza		plaza
ὑπερβολή	hyperbole			hyperbola
φαντασία	phantasy			fancy

The limits of space forbid us to give long lists of words used in various fields of thought, but we may give selected examples. In the relationships of the family, all but the very commonest terms are taken from Latin: *family* is from *familia* 'household,' *ancestor* is from *antecessor* 'predecessor'; *parent, descendant, relative, connection* are obvious Latin words; *uncle* is *avunculus* 'mother's brother' (though etymologically it means 'little grandfather'), *aunt* is *amita* 'father's sister,' *cousin* is *consobrinus* 'child of a mother's sister,' *nephew* and *niece* are from *nepos* 'grandson' and *neptis* 'granddaughter' with a shift in the meaning. Even *grand* in *grandfather* is a Latin word, for *grandfather* is a half-translation of French *grand-père;* English has extended the *grand* to *grandson*, which is quite illogical, for *grand* in *grand-père* gives the idea of age, and French *petit-fils* 'little son' gives the proper contrast, rather than our *grandson*.

Religion itself bears a Latin name, which seems to mean *diligence* and *reverence* toward the gods or toward God, as opposed to *negligence*, all of which are Latin words. The *minister*, or 'servant,' is often called the *rector* 'ruler' or the *pastor* 'shepherd'; *deacon, priest,* and *bishop*

[63]

mean respectively 'servant,' 'elder,' and 'over-seer,' in the Greek from which they come. Our *church* is a building 'pertaining to the Lord,' and our *cathedral* is the 'seat' of the bishop. *Saints* are those who have been *consecrated*, and *martyrs* are 'witnesses.' Many other words applying to the ideas of religion were mentioned above, among the Anglo-Saxon borrowings from the classics; but we must leave to Anglo-Saxon itself the credit for the words *God, heaven* and *hell, worship,* and *sin.*

Government with its *treasurer* and its *chambers* of *parliament* must be credited to Greek, though three of the four words have Latin suffixes attached; but of other common words of government, few are Anglo-Saxon except *king* and *queen, earl, lord* and *lady, knight, sheriff, kingdom,* and *folk.* The rest are Latin: whether *empire* or *republic,* the *state,* with its *executive, judicial,* and *legislative officials,* its *army* and its *police, lieutenants* and *captains* included, would have other names if there had been no Latin language. *Courts* may be *federal* or only for the *county* or *city,* the *administration* may be *democratic* or *republican, conservative* or *liberal* or *radical* or *unionist;* the *party representatives* may be *senators* or *deputies* — still all is Latin. Whether

[64]

the *people* are *subject* and, let us hope, *loyal* to a *president* or to an *emperor* as their *legal ruler*, and whether his *successor* be *elected* or *hereditary*, they are subject to Latin in their vocabulary. And a *sovereign* is a *supranus* 'one who is *supra* or over'; but the spelling was wrongly reformed to make it an apparent derivative of *reign*, which comes from the noun *regnum* 'reign' and the verb *regnare* 'to reign.' *Monarchies* and *democracies*, with other *archies* and *ocracies*, are alike Greek, while *constitutions*, *treaties*, *unions*, and *peace* are Latin; *war* is a true old Teutonic or Germanic word, though the Romans were both *bellicose* and *pugnacious*. *Titles* and *dignities* are chiefly of Latin origin; in addition to those already quoted, the *duke* is a *dux* 'leader,' the *count* is a *comes* 'companion,' the *squire* was a *scutarius* 'shield-bearer'; to which we may add the *chancellor*, the *councillor*, and the *secretary*, the *major*, the *colonel*, and the *general*, the *instructor*, the *professor*, and the *provost* or *prefect*.

We could continue these examples almost indefinitely; but more than enough has been said to show the dominance of Roman ideas in the religion and the government of the English-speaking peoples. This means, in other words, that religion and government, in the forms which persisted among speakers of English, came to those speakers of English through the agency of speakers of Latin or of languages derived from Latin. We owe them also the development and determination of many terms of relationship; and in these three fields, the family, religion, and government, we have the solid basis on which our civilization rests. For the gifts of Rome, testified to by these Latin derivatives in English, we can never be adequately grateful.

Most of the common terms applying to the sky and the weather, the parts of the body, garments, the common actions, the ordinary animals and birds, and native plants, are derived from Anglo-Saxon, as well as many terms pertaining to buildings and their parts and furnishings; yet even in these groups we find such familiar words as *season* and *autumn*, *nerve* and *muscle*, *belt* and *veil*, *impel* and *prevent*, *mule* and *eagle*, *pine* and *poplar*, *wall*, *kitchen*, and *kettle* — all from Latin, and *air*, *stomach*, *pantaloons*, *monkey*, *peach* and *cherry*, *chimney* and *desk* — these from Greek. *Chair*, *plate*, *dish*, and *cup* are Greek, and *table* and *fork* are Latin; only *knife* and *spoon* are left for native Anglo-Saxon.

But let us turn now, with some detail, into the realm of weights and measures. The τάλαν- τον was a unit of weight and value to the ancient Greek; to-day we say *a man of talent* in a figurative sense. The coin δραχμή, literally 'handful,' gives us *drachm* and *dram*. From *pecu* 'cattle' as unit of value, the Roman said *pecunia* 'money,' and we say *pecuniary;* English *fee* has the same development of meaning, since it originally meant 'cattle,' even as the cognate *Vieh* in German still does. *Capital* is an adjective derived from *caput* 'head,' and *interest* denotes the 'difference,' though the word is not used in this meaning in Latin: *debts* or *debits*, and *credits*, are 'things owed' and 'things entrusted,' *debita* and *credita*. The *libra* or 'pound' gives the French *livre*, the Italian *lira*, and the £ which is the abbreviation of the English pound. The *solidus* or 'solid' gold piece gives the French *sou*, the Italian *soldo*, and (with a suffix) the word *soldier*, originally a mercenary who fought for money. The *denarius*, a coin of 'ten' *asses*, is responsible for the English *d*, for 'penny.' French *centime* and Italian *centesimo* are *centensimus* 'hundredth'; American *cent* is a shortening of *centime*, and *dime* is a French

[67]

form of *decima* 'tenth.' The Roman normally omitted the word *libra* and said, for example, *decem pondo* 'ten by weight'; from this comes English *pound*. The *uncia* or 'unit' was one twelfth of a *libra;* this gives both *ounce* and *inch*. *Palma* and *digitus* 'finger' give *palm* and *digit; cubitus* was borrowed as *cubit*, or translated by *ell*. The *passus* 'stretch, double pace,' gives *pace*, and *mille passus* 'thousand paces,' with omission of the second word, as is usual in Latin, gives us *mile*. *Million* is an Italian augmentative of *mille* 'thousand'; *billion, trillion*, and higher numerals are obvious formations from the Latin numerals and *million*. A *quart* is a 'fourth' part, *quarta*, of a gallon; a *pint* is a 'marked' part, *pincta* (for earlier *picta*), of a larger measure. *Bushel* comes from a late word *bustellus*, probably a diminutive of the Greek πυξίς. The metric units *meter, gram, liter* are taken from μέτρον 'measure,' γράμμα 'letter, also a weight,' λίτρα 'pound' (the Greek form of the Latin *libra*); multiples are expressed by prefixing Greek numerals, as in *dekameter, hectometer, kilometer, myriameter*, and the fractions by prefixing Latin, as in *decimeter, centimeter, millimeter*. The *are* or metric unit of surface is from Latin *area*.

Our names for the months all come from Latin,
where the forms were *Januarius*, *Februarius*,
Martius, *Aprilis*, *Maius*, *Junius*, *Julius*, *Augustus*, *September*, *October*, *November*, *December*.
The Roman year originally began with March
1, which explains the numerals in September
and the later months, and in the older names
Quinctilis and *Sextilis*, which were renamed in
honor of Julius Caesar and Augustus Caesar respectively. About 150 B.C., the beginning of
the year was changed to January; but the
older system had its survivals, for March 25
remained the first day of the year in Scotland
until 1600, and in England until 1751. The
names of the days of the week originated in the
Orient, where they were considered each to be
under the influence of a heavenly body; in their
transfer from country to country, they became
the Latin *Solis dies*, *Lunae dies*, *Martis dies*,
Mercurii dies, *Jovis dies*, *Veneris dies*, *Saturni
dies*. We keep the name of the Roman deity
in *Saturday*, and translate the others, using the
Sun and the Moon, and the Teutonic gods *Tiw*,
Woden, *Thor*, *Frig*, in *Sunday*, *Monday*, *Tuesday*,
Wednesday, *Thursday*, *Friday*. As for the *cal-
endar*, the word comes from Latin *Kalendarium*,
a money-lender's account-book, so-called be-

cause interest payments were due on the *Kalendae* or first day of the months.

Let us next consider the list of subjects of study pursued in the college department of one of our largest universities. We omit names of languages, and find that *business law, drawing,* and the second word in *public speaking* are English, and that the following are of classical origin (Greek in capitals) : *accounting, AESTHETICS, ANTHROPOLOGY, ARCHITECTURE, AS-TRONOMY, BACTERIOLOGY, BIBLE, BOTANY, CHEMISTRY, commerce, ECO-NOMICS, education, ETHICS, finance, fine arts, GEOGRAPHY, GEOLOGY, HISTORY, HYGIENE, industry, LOGIC, MATHEMAT-ICS, METALLURGY, MUSIC, PHI-LOSOPHY, PHYSICal education, PHYSICS, POLITICal science, PSYCHOLOGY, public (speaking), socioLOGY, transportation, ZO-OLOGY. Miner-al-OGY* is Celtic + Latin + Greek. The totals are English $2\frac{1}{2}$, Latin $9\frac{1}{3}$, Greek $23\frac{5}{8}$, Celtic $\frac{1}{3}$.

The titles of the teaching staff of the Medical School of the same university include the following words : *ANATOMY, applied, BACTERI-OLOGY, BOTANY, CHEMISTRY, CLIN-ICal, comparative, DERMATOLOGY, DIE-*

TETICS, diseases, EMBRYOLOGY, general, gen-ito-urinary, GYNAECOLOGY, HISTOLOGY, jurisprudence, LARYNGOLOGY, materia medica, medicine, mental, METALLURGY, NEU-ROLOGY, NEUROPATHOLOGY, obstetrICS, OPHTHALMOLOGY, ORTHOPEDIC, OS-TEOLOGY, OTOLOGY, PATHOLOGY, ped-IATRICS, PHARMACY, PHYSICal educa-tion, PHYSIOLOGY, PRACTICE, research, RHINOLOGY, roentgen*OLOGY, SURGERY, THERAPEUTICS, THERAPY, TROPICal, TOXICOLOGY.* These words are exclusively *classical,* and mostly Greek; the only non-classical elements are the *d* of *applied,* the plural *s* in five words, the German name *Roentgen* in *roentgenology,* and the word *ease* in *diseases,* which is of uncertain origin, though possibly Latin.

These lists of branches of learning and of sciences prepare us to find that the technical terminology of the various sciences is mainly drawn from Latin and Greek. Let us start with *Botany.* The botanists long ago decided that for clearness' sake every plant should have a Latin name, in two parts, the first denoting the *genus* or a small group of closely related plants, and the second denoting the *species* or

[71]

particular kind. The name of the species is an adjective or a genitive modifying the name of the genus; thus the white oak is *Quercus alba*, and the cow-oak is *Quercus Michauxii*, the specific name coming from the name of a person. Irrespective of his mother-tongue, and irrespective of any peculiar names given to the trees, or of any transfers of the usual names to other trees, the botanist knows *Quercus alba* and *Quercus Michauxii* beyond possibility of error. Similarly, larger groups of plants, such as the *families*, have Latin names; examples are *Cruciferae* 'crossbearers' or mustards, *Compositae* 'composite flowers,' and with the most common ending *Violaceae* 'the violet family,' *Rosaceae* 'the rose family.' It is also agreed among botanists that the discoverer of a plant shall publish *in Latin* an accurate description of it, if his account is to be recognized as valid; for a Latin description has a definiteness and internationality which is not given by any modern language. But even the English terminology of botany is almost entirely drawn from Greek and Latin: a glossary of 726 botanical terms shows Latin 485, or 67 percent; Greek 154, or 21 percent; Latin and Greek *hybrids* 29, or 4 percent; English 58, or 8 percent.

Hybrids, we should remark, are words of which the different parts come from different languages, as in *nectari-form*, *mitri-form*, *thalami-florous*, which are Greek plus Latin. Thus of the ordinary botanical terminology, 92 percent come from the classical languages; of rarer terms, doubtless an even higher percentage would belong there.

In *Pharmacology*, drugs are known by Latin names, often the same as those˙ of the plants from which they come; and prescriptions are written in Latin. The use of Latin removes all doubt as to what is meant, for the Latin words have a fixed and unchanging significance to pharmacists over all the world.

The terminology of *Anatomy* had become a hopeless jungle of some 30,000 terms in various languages; but about 1890 an international commission was formed, which labored for eight years and reduced their number to 4,500, all in Latin form, many of them being Latinized Greek. Their international intelligibility, as well as their reduced number, has been a great boon to anatomists. But éven the commonly known terms of this science are from the classics, such as *cranium, epidermis, larynx, iris, retina*, from Greek, and *cerebrum, cerebellum, uvula*,

[73]

digit, pupil, biceps, vertebra, sternum, femur, tibia, umerus, appendix, from Latin.

Zoölogy uses the classics almost precisely as does Botany. Every animal, from man to amoeba, has a Latin name of two parts: the cat is *Felis domestica,* the lion is *Felis leo,* the tiger is *Felis tigris,* the leopard is *Felis pardus,* the puma is *Felis concolor.* The advantage of the Latin naming is seen in the case of the last animal, which is called also *cougar, catamount, painter, panther, mountain lion, American lion,* etc. Families of animals are known by such terms as *Felidae* 'cat family,' *Ursidae* 'bear family,' etc. Most of the descriptive terms also come from the same sources. From Latin *vorare* 'to eat,' we find *carnivorous* 'flesh-eating,' *herbivorous* 'grass-eating,' *graminivorous* 'grain-eating,' *insectivorous* 'insect-eating,' *omnivorous* 'eating everything.' *Digitigrade* means 'walking on the toes,' and *plantigrade* means 'walking on the soles of the feet'; *dekapod, gastropod, myriapod* contain the Greek *pod* 'foot,' and *coleoptera, hemiptera, lepidoptera* contain the Greek *pter* 'wing.'

Chemistry has another similar classical terminology; but let us limit ourselves to the names of the elements, as given in the last edi-

tion of Webster's *New International Dictionary*.
Of 82 names of elements, and two alternative
names, 42 are of Greek origin, 20 are from Latin,
12 are words chiefly personal or place names,
from various languages, but dressed up with a
Latin ending; 5 are native English, 4 are German, 1 is Swedish. Of these perhaps only 31
are familiarly known outside of technical circles;
these are *arsenic, calcium, chlorine, copper, helium,
hydrogen, iodine, magnesium, manganese, nitro-
gen, oxygen, phosphorus, platinum*, from Greek
(13); *aluminum, carbon, mercury, radium, sili-
con, sodium, sulphur*, from Latin (7); *gold, iron,
lead, silver, tin*, from English (5); *potassium*,
from English, with a Latin ending (1); *bis-
muth, cobalt, nickel, · zinc*, from German (4);
tungsten, from Swedish (1). But when the
chemist is doing technical work, he changes the
English *gold, iron, lead, silver, tin* to the Latin
aurum, ferrum, plumbum, argentum, stannum;
he transforms Latin *antimony* and *mercury* and
Greek *copper* into the Latinized Greek *stibium,
hydrargyrum, cuprum;* he makes over *potassium,
sodium, tungsten* into *kalium, natrium, wolfram-
ium*, which are Sanskrit, Greek, German respectively, with the addition of a Latin ending.
It is from this list that he makes his technical

[75]

abbreviations, such as H_2O to mean water, because one molecule of water contains two atoms of Hydrogen and one atom of Oxygen. In this technical list of elements, 61 have Latin nominative endings, 7 have Greek nominative endings, 10 are slightly altered from the Latin or Greek form, 4 are German; yet this is the list used by every English-speaking scientist, and the convenience of its uniformity and invariability is so great that, as with botanical and zoölogical nomenclature, any attempt to change it is unthinkable.

The examination of other special vocabularies gives the same results, namely that almost all technical terms are derived from Latin and Greek and not from native English words. We have seen also that familiar fields, such as religion and government, and even family relationship, are filled with words coming from the classics; and that many monosyllables owe their source to Greek and Latin. Many pairs of synonyms exist, in which one word is classical and the other is Anglo-Saxon; in other instances, one and the same Latin or Greek word has given us two or more English words, usually of different meanings. We now turn to the influence of Greek and Latin on word-formation in English.

VIII. PREFIXES

THERE are times when a language has to express new ideas, or to discriminate between similar ideas. Then any one of several things may happen. The language may borrow words from other languages, as when English took *bishop* and *priest*, *lion* and *tiger*, from the classics; or it may give new meanings to old words. The English colonists, for example, gave to the birds which they found in America names which they had used in England, such as *robin* and *blackbird*, because the red breast of the one and the black plumage of the other reminded them of the English birds, although those were really quite different; perhaps, too, they used the old names partly from that homesick longing which led them to give to their settlements in the wilderness the names of the cities which they had left behind, *Boston* and *Chester*, New *York* and New *London*.

But this method produces merely new meanings, not new words. A third way is the forming of compound words, by the union of stems

previously used, but not in the particular combination now employed ; thus English says *highway* and *woodshed*, made of good Anglo-Saxon
words, but not united into single words until
after the Norman Conquest. We find also similar compounds of Latin stems, as in *equipoise*
and *omnipresent*, and of Greek stems, as in *panorama* and *phonograph*. English even makes
compounds which are still written as two words,
or more : we write a *city man* in two words, and
a *countryman* in one ; we name one bird a *wood
thrush* and another a *woodcock;* a newspaper
writer heads an item *Peggy Johnson Camp Shoot-
ing Probe Ends*, in which the first five words
form logically one compound noun — and if the
last word had been *End* instead of *Ends*, it also
would have belonged to the compound. For
these groups of words are truly compounds, not
groups of adjectives and nouns, since the words
city and *wood* and the rest are not adjectives at
all.

As in nature there are hybrids, so among
compound words we find hybrids, words composed of parts coming from different languages,
as has been said before. A man may know that
a mule is a hybrid animal, but he perhaps does
not know that the *automobile* which has replaced

[78]

his mule has a hybrid name, Greek plus Latin, nor that when he speaks of a *radio-gram* he is talking Latin plus Greek, and that *country-man* is Latin plus English. He may need to be reminded that *be-siege* is an English prefix plus a Latin stem, and that a *super-man* is a Latin prefix plus an English stem. It is the same with suffixes: *scarce-ness* is Latin plus English, *martyr-dom* is Greek plus English, *talk-ative* is English plus Latin, *music-al* is Greek plus Latin, *huntr-ess* is English plus Greek, *colon-ize* is Latin plus Greek, *mac-adam-iz-ation* is Celtic plus Hebrew plus Greek plus Latin. Hybrid words, though often frowned upon by purists, are much more common than is generally realized.

Let us now limit ourselves for a time to the prefixes seen in English words. Of the countless Latin words which came into English, a great number were already equipped with prefixes, such as *abduct, adduce, conduct, deduct, deduce, induce, produce, reduce, seduce, traduce,* all being compounds of the verb *ducere* 'to lead.' So many such words, indeed, came into the English vocabulary, that the language has in great part changed its way of making new words by prefixes, and now is more likely, in making a new word, to use the Latin elements than to use the

Anglo-Saxon. We have made the words *co-director*, *sub-contractor*, *transatlantic*, from Latin material, and have no fear that they will fail to be understood. Beside this, many Latin compounds have in large part replaced good old Anglo-Saxon words: *pre-dict* is more often used than *fore-tell*, and other similar pairs are *pre-cursor* and *fore-runner*, *super-vision* and *over-sight*, *il-legal* and *un-lawful*.

Among our words are, however, many which would not be recognized by Caesar or by Cicero, because the combinations had not been made in their days; and yet many of them would be intelligible to either of those old Romans. An *ante-chamber* is obviously a 'room before' something else; and that which is *antediluvian* clearly took place 'before the flood.' If a friend tell us some *extraordinary nonsense*, we appreciate it as a story 'lacking in sense, outside the ordinary,' and probably consider him to be speaking *extravagantly*, or in a manner 'roving beyond' the boundaries of truth. An act is *non-moral* if it is 'apart from the moral' quality, but it is *immoral* if it is actively vicious. We may *post-date* or *ante-date* a check, using Latin prefixes to indicate our actions. We may *sub-classify* the items of an inventory, or 'classify into smaller groups'; we may *declassify*, or 'remove from classification.' But if we *decapitate*, that means to 'remove the head of,' and is the same as the English *behead*. We have long understood what *ex-presidents* are, and now we know what an *ex-kaiser* is. A *vice-president*, too, has a Latin prefix which means 'in the place of.' Our *coevals* are those 'of the same age'; since the two sexes have begun to go to school together, we have had *co-education*, and a college woman, having at last been admitted to higher education, usurps the *co* to the exclusion of her male predecessor, and is a *co-ed*. A *super-man* is 'a man of a superior kind,' even as a *super-submarine* is an under-sea boat of a superior kind, with a curious seeming contradiction in the literal meaning of the *super-sub*, as in the *New Old South Church* in Boston. A *misalliance* is an 'alliance with an inferior,' for *mis* is here developed from Latin *minus* 'less'; but a natural confusion with a native English prefix *mis*, meaning 'wrongly,' caused Latin *mis* to have the meaning 'wrongly' in *miscount*, *misnomer*, and some others. *Mischance* was even halfway translated into English as *mishap*, and *perchance*, a phrase meaning originally 'by chance,' but now meaning 'possibly,' was halfway anglicized

[81]

into *perhaps; hap* must be credited to Scandinavian, however, rather than to Anglo-Saxon. If we wish to denote a repetition of an action, we prefix *re*, as in *remake* 'to make again'; but this same prefix meant in Latin not only 'again,' but 'back, backward,' and some of our words have come down to us from older times. When there are two words seemingly identical, a hyphen is set in the new word, so that we *re-coil* a rope, but *recoil* from a peril, and *re-form* the broken ranks, but *reform* politics. There is a further difference, too, that the new words have a slight secondary stress on the first syllable, for distinction, as one will see by reading the last sentence aloud; and he will make the same variation in expressing a desire to have a damaged umbrella *re-covered* and a lost umbrella *recovered*. Curiously, the word *cover* is not identical with the second part of *recover*, for the former comes from Latin *cooperire* and the latter from Latin *recuperare;* but the English derivatives have become identical, except for the prefixed *re*.

Of all the words quoted in the last paragraph, only the Latin ancestor of *recover* was used by Caesar and by Cicero; the ancestor of our verb *reform* may have greeted the ears of Virgil, but probably did not; the other words are all of very late formation, many of them within the memory of those who may read these pages. But English, as we have said, is stocked also with many words which, like *recover*, have come down to us from the Latin of Caesar and Cicero; in the vocabulary of the former are the words which give us *abject* 'thrown away,' [14] *admit* 'let go to or toward,' *concourse* 'a running together,' *deport* 'to carry away,' *except* 'taken out,' *preterit* 'gone by.' There are hundreds and thousands of others, some of which were used by the authors whose works we read in school, others of which were not used by them, either through mere chance or else because they were made at a later date, even as English *highway* and *woodshed*, though made of old Anglo-Saxon elements, seem not to have been used as actual compound words until after the Anglo-Saxon period. *Omnipotent* comes from a good old Latin word, but *omnipresent* comes from a word first used centuries after the beginning of the Christian era. It makes no difference to us to-day that the one word is older than the other; but we may wonder, for example, whether *sub-acid* really comes from Latin *subacidus* 'somewhat acid,' or has been made in modern times,

[83]

as we have made *sub-globular* and *sub-rigid* and other words, to indicate the possession of a quality in an imperfect or smaller degree. And again, we have such a word as *sojourn*, which comes through the French from a Latin *sub-diurnare* 'to remain through the day,' which is not actually found in any Latin text, but the existence of which is clearly implied by the French word. It matters not at what date the words were compounded, interesting as their histories may be; they are composed of Latin elements, and are as truly part of our debt to the Latin language as though they had fallen trippingly from the lips of Cicero against Catiline.

In many instances, the prefixes are disguised by changes which took place in Latin itself. For example, the prefix *sub* 'under' may appear unchanged, as in *sub-stitute*, or it may suffer alterations of its final consonant, as it does in *suc-cess*, *suf-frage*, *sug-gest*, *sup-position*, *su-spect;* and a form which borrowed an *s* from the preposition and prefix *ex*, survives in *sus-pend*, *sus-tain*, *sur-reptitious*. Not infrequently the prefix underwent changes in French, and that is why we say *contra-dict*, as in Latin, and *counter-mand* and *counter-feit*, as in French. *Pro-tractus* 'drawn forth' gives us *protract*, like the Latin, and *portrait*, like the French; but one word refers to drawing forth in time, and the other to drawing forth from the living object to a canvas. French is responsible, too, for a confusion of the Latin prefix *dis* 'apart' with *de* 'from'; we easily distinguish *dis-pel* and *de-sist*, but we know that *de-face* is really *dis-face*, only because the history of the word is known far enough back to show that it has the same prefix which we see also in *dis-pel* and in *di-lapidate*.

The disguises which the prefixes assume are sometimes almost impenetrable. Our *abbreviate* and our *abridge* both come from one Latin word, *abbreviare;* but the prefix is not *ab* 'from,' for the word means 'to bring *ad breve*, to a short form,' and it is merely the euphonic change of *d* to *b* before *b* which misleads us. *Anti-cipate* contains not the Greek *anti* 'against,' but the Latin *ante* 'before,' as its meaning shows. *An-cestor* contains this same *ante*, for the word goes back to *antecessor* 'predecessor,' shortened by its development in French. Latin *con-suetudo* 'habit,' with a familiar prefix, gives us through French both *costume* and *custom*, wherein the prefix is invisible; oddly, our word *habit*, itself a Latin word, unites the meanings of both deriv-

[85]

atives of *consuetudo*. The participle *renegatus* 'denied' gives us not only the obvious *renegade*, but also *runagate;* for the popular fancy transformed the strange *renegade* to *runne a gate* 'run on the road, be a vagabond.' We can hardly realize that the same Latin verb gives us to *renig* at cards, though the more literary spelling *renege* may help our understanding. Latin *adventura* 'thing about to happen' became French *aventure*, but English replaced the *d* in *adventure* after it took the word from French. This is only to 'lean backward,' so to speak, even as when we say *dismiss* and *disrupt*, restoring the *s* of the prefix, though Latin had lost it in *di-missus* and in *di-ruptus;* but we sometimes do even worse, and give to a word an apparent prefix which it never had either in Latin or in French : English made *ad-vance* out of French *avancer*, as though it were like French *aventure*, which had formerly begun with *ad;* but *avancer* never had the prefix *ad,* for it was a derivative of *ab* + *ante*. *Admiral* does not contain *ad,* either, but is a shortening of Arabic *amīr-el-bahr* 'prince of the sea,' somewhat confused with Latin *admirabilis*. Neither does *alligator* contain *ad,* despite such words as *al-literate* and *al-lude,* for it is really the Spanish *el lagarto*

[86]

de Indias 'the lizard of the Indies,' shortened and changed to look and sound like a Latin word. But to end this list with a real Latin prefix, *sir-loin* stands for *super-loin*, with *super* in its French form *sur*, as in *surprise* and *sur-mount;* but in *sirloin* the *sur* has somehow become *sir*, which started the fanciful story that this cut of meat was knighted because of its excellence.

Greek prefixes are not so common in English as are the Latin prefixes. They are to be seen, however, in many common words, such as *apo-stle* 'sent from,' *cata-strophe* 'turning down, upsetting,' *cat-hedral* 'place of sitting down,' *cat-holic* 'according to the whole,' *dia-meter* 'measure through.' *Syn-tax* was translated by the Romans as *construction*, and we have taken both words; and there are other similar pairs, such as *synchronous* and *contemporary*, *sympathy* and *compassion*, where the differences of meaning are slight or non-existent. When we employ Greek prefixes to-day in making new words, they are used almost exclusively in combination with other Greek stems, and form rather highly technical words, in most instances, such as *pro-ethnic* and *hypo-sulphite*. There is one exception: we use *anti* freely to make words like *anti-American, anti-suffrage, anti-imperialism,* so

[87]

that a person who is known to be an opponent of proposed measures is likely to be called an *anti*, without more ado, much as though we called him, in good Anglo-Saxon, an *against-er* — but we don't; we take refuge in Greek, rather than use the inherited resources of English.

One other Greek prefix should be mentioned, and that is the so-called *alpha privative*, which appears as *a* before consonants and as *an* before vowels: *a-byss* 'that which has no bottom,' *an-archy* 'no rule,' *an-ecdote* 'not edited.' It is equivalent in meaning to Latin *in* in *in-human*, *im-mature*, and to English *un* in *un-belief*, *un-lawful*. We must not confuse this Latin *in* with another Latin *in*, which means 'in,' as in *innate* and *induce*. This second Latin *in* is hard to distinguish from the Anglo-Saxon *in* of the same meaning: *inbred* and *inland* were used in Anglo-Saxon, and have the native suffix. But if we cannot trace the history of the word back to the time when Latin and English had not joined forces, we can rely on only one criterion; the Anglo-Saxon prefix does not change its *n* before certain consonants, but keeps it unchanged, as in *inbred* and *inborn*, which, if Latin, would change the *n* to *m*, as in *imbue*. In many instances, no decision can be reached, even as is the case with the prefix *mis*, already mentioned; but in view of the general use of Latin prefixes, it is likely that the *in* in most instances comes from Latin.

We have been speaking, in the main, of prefixes which are still in use to form new words; they are appropriately known as *living* or *productive* suffixes. Most of the Latin and of the Greek prefixes are in fact still living in English, even if only in technical uses; only a few of them are now *unproductive* or *dead*. Among these is *for*, found only in *for-feit* and in *fore-close*, not to be confused with the equally dead Anglo-Saxon prefix *for* in *forbid*, *forsake*, and some other words, nor with a different Anglo-Saxon *fore*, seen in *fore-head* and in *fore-word*, still used in making new words. The Latin *for* is from the adverb *foris* 'outside,' so that *forfeit*, being for *foris factum*, means 'put outside,' and *foreclose* means 'shut outside.' The dead prefixes are of importance to us only for the words which they have made; but the living prefixes are of value to us for the words which they have made, for those which they are now making, and for those which they are hereafter to make. For this reason, the Latin and Greek prefixes are of the utmost importance to the user of English, as one of the chief means by which new words are made. The manner in which they have largely usurped the functions of the native Anglo-Saxon prefixes should be clear, if not from the discussion in the present chapter, at any rate from the examples given in the notes.[15]

Many of these prefixes we use with the utmost freedom, forming with their aid words which may never be used again, merely because no one happens to feel the need of expressing the same idea again in the same way: so we hear or read of the *extra-curricular* activities of our college students, and of their *inter-fraternity* agreements, of shirts with the merit of *pre-shrunk* neckbands, of those persons who, in respect to the foreign loans, are *anti-cancellationists;* even of a defendant in court who demands a *super-jury* to try him, and a haberdasher who claims that his clothes for men have *super-values*. Yet although the words are entirely new to us, we understand them with ease, never being tempted to look for them in the dictionaries, where, as we instinctively realize, they would not be found. The machinery of word formation by Latin and Greek prefixes has become part and parcel of our mother tongue.

IX. SUFFIXES

IF Latin and Greek prefixes are important in the forming of new words in English, the Latin and Greek suffixes are even more so. It is hard to realize, perhaps, that *talkative* and *flirtatious* owe their endings to Latin, and that *flapperitis* has a Greek suffix, while a *dancery* and an *eatery* are under obligations to both tongues. Non-literary the last three examples may be, but they are words readily formed and readily understood, which proves the living quality of their suffixes: for suffixes, like prefixes, are to be divided into *living* and *dead*, or *productive* and *non-productive*, according to whether they may or may not still be used to form new words.

One of our commonest suffixes is the Latin *tor*, in *doctor*, originally meaning 'teacher,' *inventor* 'finder,' and countless others. When this was added to verbs of the first Latin conjugation, the stems of which end in a characteristic *a*, the combination *ator* was formed, which we have in such words as *operator* and *equator;* and the combination was extended to other words in English, especially where there is a corresponding English verb ending in *ate;* so one perambulates in a *perambulator* and separates with a *separator*. An *auxiliator* is used to help the reluctant growth of the hair on one's head, or to induce an automobile engine to do more effective work; but the word has not yet reached the dictionary, and the verb *auxiliate* has gone out of use. There is even a *Kelvin-ator*, for domestic refrigeration without the use of ice; it was so named because Lord Kelvin was an eminent authority on temperatures.

In the last word, our ending was added to a non-classical stem, which could not lay claim to a first conjugation *a;* and we note also that several of these words are applied not to persons, but to machines, which is a common shift of meaning in words denoting the agent. The activity of *ator* was not however confined to these limits; for through the French it became *or*, which was confused with an Anglo-Saxon ending *er*, of the same meaning, and an Anglo-Saxon *sailer*, if a man, became changed to a *sailor*, though his boat still remains a *sailer*. In revenge, many a Latin word lost its *or* in favor of *er*, as when *fundator* became *founder* and not

[92]

foundor; but other words, like *donor* from *dona-tor*, retained the *or* which was rightfully theirs.

To this masculine ending *tor* there was a feminine ending *trix*, as in *executor* and *executrix;* but most of the *trix* words have been formed in comparatively recent times, for the older words changed their ending to *ess*, which started out as Greek *issa* and reached us through Latin and French. With its aid we say *actress* and *protectress*, corresponding to *actor* and *protector*, which are Latin words; and without the intervening *tor* we have *prophetess*, which is all Greek, *princess*, which is half Latin, and *shepherdess*, which is English with the Greek suffix.

Three Latin suffixes form abstracts in English : *ation, ity, ment.* [16] A Latin suffix *tio*, varying with *sio*, appears in such inherited words as *action, question, excursion, oration*. In the last example, it has been, like *tor*, associated with the *a* of the first conjugation, and in this form we use it with English bases in *flirtation* and *starvation*, especially as we have such combinations as *condemn* and *condemnation*, inherited from Latin. *Ty* or *ity* is seen in the old words *liberty* and *capacity*, and in the later words, not known to classical Latin, *improbability, sociability*, and *scarcity;* it even makes its way into

[93]

oddity, with a Scandinavian base, and into *work-ability* and *sal-ability*, which are English roots with a double Latin suffix. But sometimes its sway is disputed by the Anglo-Saxon *ness*, as in *sociableness* and *scarceness; oddness* and *oddity*, however, differ somewhat in meaning, for *oddness* is never *concrete*, while *oddity* is often used to mean an 'odd thing.' Abstract nouns are in fact very likely to shift their meanings to concrete objects, as when *habitation* comes to mean not an 'act of dwelling,' but a 'house,' and *humanity* may mean either 'the state of being humane or human,' or 'human beings in general.' Our third suffix, *ment*, is found in *ferment* and *torment*, and with English bases in *wonderment* and *atonement;* the last does really mean being 'at one' with God, even as an illiterate preacher not seldom pronounces it. The English speak of *oddments*, which seems to combine *odds and ends* with the ending of *fragments* and the meaning of *remnants;* they say *fitments*, as a mixture of *fittings* and *equipment*. A recent novelist writes *vanishment* and *relaxment* — possibly feeling that *relaxation* had acquired too definitely a special meaning of vacation freedom from work, while he wished to indicate a physical freedom from tension.

Another ending which formed Latin abstracts
was *ia*, which was the ending of the Latin originals of *militia, grace, discord, modesty*, despite
their differences. [17] This was not productive in
English, except in combination with the present
participle. The stem of the Latin present participle ended in *ant* or *ent*, which comes into
English without change, as in *vigilant* and *convenient*, which are used as adjectives; it gives
also some substantives, like *agent* and *regent*.
Among them are some which had *ent* in Latin,
but have *ant* in English : *remnant* from *remanens*,
assistant from *assistens*, *servant* from *serviens;*
for in French the two endings were pronounced
alike, and were therefore spelled alike, unless a
knowledge of the Latin originals caused a res-
toration of the Latin spelling, as it did in most
words. Returning to our *ia*, we find it com-
bined with the participial stem to make *antia*
and *entia*, which appear in English in two forms :
significance and *flagrancy, convenience* and *expe-
diency;* a few examples show the *a* in defiance
of the Latin, as in *assistance* and *resistance*,
though we have *persistence* and *subsistence*. It
is curious to find some words with *nce* and others
with *ncy,* and the explanation of the latter leads
us to Greek. Greek had abstracts ending in *ia*,

[95]

from which we have *comedy* and *tragedy*, and numerous other words. This Greek *ia* was accented on the *i*, as in *harmonía;* but the similar Latin words were accented on the antepenult, as in *violéntia*. Many of the Greek words came into late Latin, keeping their accents, and affected the accent of some Latin words; thus *modéstia*, with the Latin accent, became Italian *modéstia*, but *modestía*, with the Greek accent, became French *modestie*, while *injúria*, with the Latin accent, became French *injure*. In this way words like *grace* and *romance* represent in English the Latin accent, and *modesty*, *injury*, and *flagrancy* represent the Greek accent; and we take *dependence* from French — it has no classical Latin original — and give it a parallel form *dependency*, we make *reliance* and *conveyance* from Latin materials, we make *hindrance* and *forbearance* from English roots.

This Greek ending *ia*, though not itself productive in English, was through its accent the chief factor in forming an English suffix *ry* or *ery*. Latin had many adjectives ending in *arius*, from which we have, for example, *primary* and *ordinary;* [18] the feminine *ária*, remade to *aría* by the influence of the Greek accent, developed into *ery* or *ry*, and we use it freely in the Latin

derivatives *distillery, archery, nursery, jewellery*
or *jewelry*, and with English bases in *robbery,
bakery, yeomanry*. The last three examples illustrate some of its various meanings, as the
'*act* of robbing,' the '*place* of baking,' 'yeomen
collectively.' The second of these meanings alone
is illustrated in the recent colloquial words *eatery,
beanery, dancery*. The Greek accent on the *i* of
the suffix is seen in Spanish *cafetería* and in
Italian *cavallería*, both of which are commonly
accented otherwise when used as English words.

Arius, in the masculine form, denotes the
followers of occupations, as in *notary* and *an-
tiquary*. With French changes, we have also
vicar, carpenter, premier, and *engineer;* and the
eer form has become productive in English, as
in *charioteer* and *auctioneer*, often with a somewhat derogatory implication, as in *pamphleteer*
and *sonneteer*. Recently, we have made the
words *profiteer* 'one who profits unduly,' and
bucketeer 'one who operates a bucket-shop, an
unscrupulous stock-broker.'

For reasons which lie in the development of
English itself, quite apart from Latin, we have
verbs and nouns which are identical in form;
one *loves* the *fire* in winter, the same person may
fire the *love* of a person of the other sex. It may

[97]

then not be so surprising that we can *complete* the *reverse* operation, as well as *reverse* [19] the *complete* operation; only, in these examples the words come from Latin perfect participles, and while some adjectives from participles have been made into verbs on the English principle, in most cases the process is based on a phenomenon of Latin itself. For Latin made additional verbs on the participial stem, and had *tracto* as well as *traho*, *pulso* as well as *pello*, with little or no difference of meaning. English took some of these pairs from Latin, *repel* and *repulse*, *revert* and *reverse*, but more often took only the participial form for use as verbs, as in *detract, elect, suspect;* and after their model it used other participles as verbs, though they were not so used in Latin, such as *duplicate* and *cogitate*, and even made other apparent participles for use solely as verbs, such as *capacitate* and *nobilitate*, and even *assassinate* and *camphorate*, the roots of which come from Asiatic languages.

In this way, Latin gives us one of our chief methods of forming new verbs; but the Latin participle gave us many adjectives as well, and some of the words with the participial ending were adjectives even in Latin, giving us *vertebrate* 'possessing a backbone,' *ovate* 'egg-shaped,'

[98]

and other words. There are also other special
endings in English, which go back to the Latin
participle. The *atus* of the first conjugation,
through a French form, gives us *ee*, as in *em-
ployee* 'one employed,' as contrasted with the
employer, and *payee*, contrasted with *payer;*
we have no fear in extending this suffix, for we
make *vendee*, meaning not 'one who is sold,' but
'one to whom a sale is made,' regardless both of
the proper meaning and of the fact that the
French participle of this word ends in *u* (*vendu*,
not *vendé*). If we wish, we can make up words
with *ee* quite freely, expecting to be readily
understood: the *talker* talks to a *talkee*, the
bore bores his *boree*.

Again, the feminine ending *ata* became *ada*
in Spanish and in Italian; from the former
language we have the *armada* which sailed
against England, and the 'snowy' state of *Ne-
vada*. *Ada* became *ade* in French, as in our
cavalcade and *crusade*, *colonnade* and *marmalade*.
The last word is really *meli-mel-ata* 'made with
honey-melons,' with *ade* as in *lemon-ade* 'made
with lemons'; and *ade* is used either as a suffix
of fruit beverages, in *orangeade*, or as a separate
word, in *raspberry ade*. But when a manu-
facturer of jams recently desired some new names

for his products, he borrowed part of *marmalade* and concocted *grapelade* and *plumlade*. In the same way, *chandel-ier* (Latin *candelarius*, derivative of *candela*) bids fair to establish a suffix *lier*, denoting lighting fixtures, for we already have *gaso-liers* and *electro-liers;* and *linoleum*, which, being made largely of *lin*seed *oil*, has a right to its name, threatens us with *leum* or *oleum* for floor coverings, since recent advertising recommends *til-oleum* and *congo-leum*, the latter name being invented by the makers of *congo roofing* when they turned their energies to floor mats. Startling as some of these words seem, they are merely employing a normal way of securing new suffixes, and the same processes are involved in such a word as *talk-ative*, with a Latin suffix attached to an English root. The ending *ivus* is attached to the participial suffix, as in *cap-t-ive, inquisitive, successive, declara-t-ive*, and the first conjugation *a* is cut off with the *tive* to form a new suffix, usable in English to form new words. *A tor* and *ation* got their *a* in the same manner, as did also the suffix *able*.

Latin *bilis* [20] made verbal adjectives, such as *invincible* 'not able to be conquered,' *navigable* 'able to be navigated,' and in combination with the first conjugation *a* gave to English the living suffix just mentioned, which we use freely in making *chargeable, serviceable, reliable* — formerly a much reviled word, since it meant 'able to be relied *on*,' needing an adverb to complete its meaning; but do we not say *laughable*, meaning 'able to be laughed *at*,' *perishable* 'able or inclined to perish' (in the active voice), *peaceable* 'inclined to peace'? Which shows that suffixes cannot be expected to stay fixed within the narrowest possible limits of meaning, and that they are much more useful if they are spread out a little.

Just as the suffix *able* (not identical with the adjective *able*, which is *habilis*, a derivative of *habeo* 'I have') has extended its range of meaning, so other endings have extended their range of use; notably the adjective endings *al, an, ous,* which began their extension in Latin, and continued it in English. Let us see first what the three were in their earlier use. *Al* comes from Latin *alis* in such words as *pedal* and *temporal,* and its neuter plural is seen in *marginalia, mammalia,* and the like, shortened in *arrival, denial, battle,* and extended to English bases in *betrothal* and *withdrawal.*

An comes from Latin *anus,* as in *urban* and *urbane, human* and *humane,* and with French

changes in *villain* and *captain*.[21] It is especially
used to form adjectives from proper names, as
in *Roman* and *European*, and has in English
practically displaced Latin *ensis* in the same use,
for our *Athenian* was a Latin *Atheniensis;* but
ensis survives in some later words like *Portuguese* and *Chinese, Bostonese* and *Carlylese*.
Modern names like *American* and *Canadian*,
Minnesotan and *Indianian*, show that *an* is still
a living suffix, and that it often takes the form
ian. The neuter plural also is used in English,
to denote a collection of books or the like:
Americana 'books on America,' *Shakespeariana*,
Byroniana.

Ous comes through the French from Latin
osus, as in *famous* and *odious*, and is attached
to an English root in *wondr-ous*. When, however, it passes direct from Latin into English,
it appears as *ose*, as in *verbose* 'wordy' and in
tuber-ose 'having a tuber or bulb,' for this word
is not etymologically either a *tube* or a *rose*.

These are the three endings, *al, an, ous*, which
extended their domains in Latin and continued
to do so in English. To show this, we must first
note that the nominative *us* disappears when
the word comes into English, as when *reverendus*
becomes *reverend, stupidus* becomes *stupid*,[22]

secondarius becomes *secondary*, *civicus* becomes *civic*. But when *serius* becomes *serious*, it is really because *serius* was in late Latin replaced by *seriosus*. The same alteration, either in Latin or in French or in English, made *carnivorous* from *carnivorus*, *pious* from *pius*, *ferocious* from *ferox*, and so on. *Al* was added to make *eternal* and *paternal* from *aeternus* and *paternus*. *An* made *Mediterranean* and *patrician* from *Mediterraneus* and *patricius*. Words in *arius* are responsible for *gregari-ous* and *librari-an;* those in *torius* and *sorius* [23] take all three endings, *notori-ous* and *censori-ous*, *pretori-an*, *professori-al* and *tonsori-al*.

A curious variety appears in the English words coming from Greek adjectives in *icus*, such as *gigantic* and *chronic*. Many, especially those denoting arts and sciences, become substantives, like *magic* and *arithmetic*, and since some of these were plurals in Greek, some of them become plurals in English, like *physics* and *athletics*. It makes some distinctively English words, like *Byronic*. But the odd thing is to see how easily *ic* amalgamates itself with our three Latin endings *al*, *an*, *ous: poetic* and *poetical* have the same meaning; *physic* is a medicine and *physician* is one who prescribes the physic, *physics* is a

[103]

science and *physical* means pertaining to that science; a *mechanic* is one who works at a machine, and *mechanical* means relating to the machine, but a *mechanic-ian* is a mechanic who knows the theory also. *Economic* means pertaining to the science *economic-s*, and *economical* means 'thrifty.'

There is also a Latin *ic*, in a few words like *civic* and *public*, *domestic* and *rustic*.[24] Its greatest importance is in the word *viaticus*, for the neuter *viaticum*, with an implied *aes* 'money,' meant 'traveling money,' and gave to French the word *voyage*, in a changed meaning. This word yielded an ending *age*, found for example in *marriage* and *courage*. When these words came into English, *voyage* being then restricted to travel by sea, the ending became very productive, giving *package* and *storage*, *cartage* and *milage*, even the *gallonage* of the gasoline dealer. But this *ic* is not that in *fic*, as in *terrific* 'making terror,' where the *fic* is a form of the root *fac* 'make'; from such compounds come verbs which in English end in *fy*, like *edify* (in which the original meaning of 'make a house' has been lost), *terrify*, *pacify*, and even the English words *dandify*, *speechify*, *Frenchify*.

When the Russian *Bolsheviki* and *Mensheviki*

became English *Bolshevists* and *Menshevists*, we attached a Greek suffix to the Russian stems; at first some writers called them *Maximalists* and *Minimalists*, but these Latin-Greek terms have disappeared. *Menshevists* have vanished politically as well as linguistically, but the *Bolshevists* still practice their *Bolshevism* and try to *bolshevize* their neighbors. All three endings are Greek; and the root also is Greek in *baptize* 'to dip,' *Baptist* 'one who dips (or believes in dipping),' *baptism* 'the act of dipping.' These endings form new words with great freedom, largely connected with professions and lines of conduct or with doctrines, as in *colonize* and *civilize*, *monopolize* and *monopolist*, *moralize* and *moralist*, *socialism* and *socialist* and the recent verb *to socialize*, *hypnotism* and *Quakerism* and *despotism*.[25] When we have both *ego-ism* and *ego-tism*, the latter word seems to owe its *t* to *despot-ism*, by a wrong division such as we have met in other words, induced by the self-will of the *ego-tist* which makes him akin to the *despot*. The verb is often spelled with *ise*, by French influence; a derivative in *ation* is common, as in *colonization* and *civilization*, and even *hospitalization* and *domicilization*, the last word not being in Webster's Dictionary.

Three more Greek suffixes are in active life in English, *ite*, *itis*, *oid*, besides some of less common use. *Ite* denotes natives of a place, as in *Moabite* and *Canaanite*, and in modern *Muscovite* and *Brooklynite;* it may be used to name adherents or partisans of a person or thing, as in *Millerite* and *Hicksite*, *bleacherite* and *navyite*. *Itis* is used by medical science to denote inflammations, as in the ancient words *nephritis* and *pleuritis*, and the modern *laryngitis* and *appendicitis*, which last word has a Latin base. A newspaper writer even coins *flapperitis* to indicate that which ails or characterizes the *flapper*. *Oid* is really the second part of Greek compound adjectives, coming from a word meaning 'shape'; we have it in *anthropoid* 'man-shaped,' *spheroid* 'sphere-shaped,' *ovoid* 'egg-shaped,' the last with a Latin base — and all these words denote imperfect resemblance, rather than perfect resemblance.

There are other suffixes coming from Latin and Greek, and found in English words; some of them are in occasional living use, others are found merely in words taken from Latin or from Greek, and are not used to form new words in English. [26] We pass them by, for we have already seen many suffixes producing new words,

[106]

even words which have appeared within our own memories, which in some cases will probably disappear within our own lifetimes.[27] Some, as we have said, are distinctly made for the occasion, "nonce-words," but these are valuable as showing the vigorous life and ready intelligibility of the suffixes. Unlike the prefixes, the suffixes show little discrimination in the bases to which they attach themselves: Latin and Greek suffixes unite with Latin or with Greek or with English stems, with much freedom, and the living suffixes of English origin [28] do likewise, while Anglo-Saxon prefixes rarely, and Greek prefixes almost never, take to themselves partners from any but their own languages.

One curious result, however, of the use of classical suffixes is that we have a preference for adjectives and abstract nouns, and for words of some other categories, coming from Latin and Greek, and that consequently we have many roots of Anglo-Saxon origin with derivatives taken from the corresponding Latin (less often Greek) root. So we say *life* and *vital*, *town* and *municipal*, *mind* and *mental*, *eye* and *ocular*, and the like ; the noun is Anglo-Saxon, and the derivatives are Latin, as are also *vitality*, *municipality*, *mentality*. Where we have both adjectives, as in *sunny* and *solar*, it is the Latin word which has the literal meaning 'pertaining to the sun,' and the Anglo-Saxon word has only derived meanings, as in a *sunny* smile, *sunny* locks, a *sunny* room. The same development is seen in *handy* and *manual*, *deadly* and *mortal*; for *handy* now means little more than 'convenient,' and *deadly* often applies to spiritual death or to sorrows, in which senses *mortal* is less used. This doubling of the number of possible derivatives has greatly increased the power of English to discriminate between similar but not identical ideas, and has made the language fuller and richer.

Enough has been said of the powers possessed in English by the suffixes of Latin and Greek origin; it is time to pass on to syntax and to actual word forms, not mere words, but words which have come into English with their inflectional or conjugational endings unchanged.

X. WORDS AND FORMS

SYNTAX must be dismissed with a brief mention. The influence of one language upon another in syntax is exceedingly difficult to analyze, the more so when the two languages are, like Latin and Anglo-Saxon, essentially similar in their usages; and there is the further problem as to how far any language actually does affect the syntax of another, for syntax resists foreign influence obstinately. In two points, however, Latin almost certainly influenced English, namely in the use of the absolute phrase and in that of the accusative and infinitive; both are illustrated in *All things considered, I thought him to be guilty*. The two constructions are perhaps native to Anglo-Saxon, but Latin influence has caused them to be more often used in English than they would have been without the foreign pressure.

If actual words attract our attention next, there is rich material. Most Latin words, in coming into English, lose their endings to some degree; but there are many which retain the endings of the nominative. In fact, every declension is represented in this way. English has such words as *formula* and *militia*, *animus* and *stimulus*, *odium* and *opprobrium*, *clamor*, *agitator*, and *tribunal*, *census* and *status*, *series* and *species*. Every one of these has kept its nominative ending; and they are but samples of a vast number of such words.[29] Some words indeed have regained their Latin endings after losing them in the meantime; *sinister* became French *sinistre* and then reverted to *sinister* in English, and words like *favor* and *honor* similarly went through an intermediate stage in French, though now they have their old Latin forms again. Some words have done even better, securing a Latin form to which they are not entitled: *neuter* comes from French *neutre*, which itself comes from the Latin *neutrum*, so that the word *neuter* in English no longer has its neuter form, but has accidentally assumed a masculine form. *Arbor*, in some rare and technical meanings, is Latin *arbor* 'tree,' but as a latticework covered with vines it is a corruption of *herbarium* 'collection or garden of plants.' Other words have in English perfectly good Latin forms, but were not used in classical Latin: *penumbra* is a late combination of *paene* 'almost' and *umbra* 'shadow'; *sanatorium* is also late Latin, and *sanitarium* is not Latin at all, but a Latinizing of *sanitary* in imitation of other words with the same ending; *realtor* is a shortening of *real estate operator*. Yet it is quite justifiable to include here the words which have been made with real Latin endings, even though they were not used in ancient times, and the words which after being changed have reverted to their ancient forms; for both classes illustrate the debt of English to Latin in the matter of actual terminations. Only words like *neuter* and *arbor*, from *neutrum* and *herbarium*, should be excluded from consideration.

Adjectives, too, as well as substantives, have been accepted by English. Among them are comparatives, like *interior* and *exterior*, and superlatives, like *maximum* and *minimum*. These examples illustrate the transfer of adjectives to use as substantives, for every one of them may be used either as an adjective or as a substantive; but, in general, the Latin adjectives which are used in English in unchanged forms have become substantives. Thus a *vacuum* is an 'empty thing,' a *serum* is a 'clear, transparent thing,' a *pendulum* is a 'swinging thing'; a *medium* once meant but a 'middle thing,' or means of accomplishing something, but has been transferred to a person who claims to be a 'middle thing' or means of communication between the dead and the living. A *nostrum* is a thing which is 'ours,' because no one else knows the secret of making it. An *album* is a 'white thing' on which something is to be written. All these words are neuter in form, because they denote things, except *medium*, which has been transferred to persons also. Of masculine forms denoting persons, we find the *miser*, whose name indicates that he is at least theoretically 'wretched,' and the *pauper*, who is 'poor' both in Latin and in English. He who is *emeritus* has *earned* and will no longer continue to earn his pay. A *bonus* means a 'good thing' in the way of an *honorarium*, but in Latin it means a 'good man,' for the gender is masculine. A *quietus* is in English a state of quiet, but in Latin it is only a masculine adjective and not an abstract. An *integer* is a 'whole' number, and has the masculine form because the word *numerus* 'number' is masculine; but an *ultima* is a 'last' syllable of a word, and is feminine, for the word *syllaba* 'syllable' is feminine. *Quadragesima* is theoretically, though not mathematically, the 'fortieth' day before Easter Day, and *dies* is in some meanings feminine. Of third

declension adjectives, apart from the comparatives already given, a *simile* is a 'like thing,' a
biceps is a 'two-headed' muscle, a stock is at
par when its price is 'equal' to its original or
theoretical value, *velox* is a photographic paper
which in comparison with its predecessors was
'quick' to receive the imprint of the negative.

There are also some participles, mainly in
the neuter form. A *dictum* is a thing 'said,' a
desideratum is a thing 'desired,' a *datum* is a
thing 'given' as a fact, an *erratum* is a thing 'mis-
taken,' a *stratum* is a thing 'spread out.' There
are a few gerundives: an *addendum* is a thing
'to be added,' a *memorandum* is a thing 'to be
recalled.' Some of these are commoner in the
plurals: *data, addenda, agenda, corrigenda, mem-
oranda;* and we should be careful not to say that
the data is before us, because *data* is a real plural
and not a singular. Occasionally, however, a
new singular is made in this fashion; our *era* is
an example. *Aes* meant 'copper, a coin, a
counter'; and the plural *aera* 'counters' became
in late Latin a singular denoting a starting-point
from which something was reckoned, which gives
English *era* with the usual change of Latin *ae*
to *e* in the body of words.

In fact, Latin plural forms are important for

English, for many words which have been taken over without change have kept their Latin plurals. We say one *alumnus* and several *alumni*, and the corresponding feminine word is *alumna*, with the plural *alumnae*. The plural of the neuters of the second declension has already been illustrated in *data* and *addenda*. The third declension gives us a variety, such as *cicatrix cicatrices*, *crux cruces*, *apex apices*, *axis axes*, *forceps forcipes*, *cognomen cognomina*, *genus genera*. *Apparatus* and *series*, representing the fourth and the fifth declensions, do duty for both numbers, in English as in Latin. Many words, of course, have both English plurals and Latin plurals, and one will sound more natural to us than the other ; *radiuses*, for example, has to the writer's ear an uncouthness from which *radii* is free, though the dictionaries give their approval to both forms. Occasionally the two plurals have different meanings : *indexes* is normally used of tables of reference in books, and *indices* is the only form used in the technical mathematical meaning ; the filaments in flower-blossoms are called *stamens*, while *stamina* in the meaning 'strength' is no longer felt as a plural of *stamen*, but has become a singular. On the other hand, while the plural of *opus* is *opera*, the word *opera* 'musical drama' is another word, a singular noun of the first declension.

Some of our English words are Latin plurals which we rarely or never use in the singular form. Besides some already mentioned, we have *minutiae, lapilli, literati, comitia, incunabula, rostra, infusoria, miscellanea, Americana* and other words in *ana, insignia, marginalia, memorabilia, paraphernalia,* and *regalia.* The familiar exclamation *jimminy* or *by jimminy* is often explained as the vocative in an exclamation, *Gemini,* the constellation of the Twins Castor and Pollux; but it is more probably a shortening of the vocative *Jesu domine* to *Je-mine.* Other case forms appear in some of our familiar words. The genitive forms the second part of *arborvitae* 'tree of life' and of *lignumvitae* 'wood of life,' and the first part of *juris-consult, juris-diction, legislator. Cornucopia* is a remodeling of *cornu copiae* 'horn of plenty,' with the genitive as the second part; the Romans and not we were responsible for the illogical remodeling. *Quorum* means those 'of whom' the number is sufficient for the transaction of business; *omnium* 'of all' is used in *omnium gatherum,* where the second word is humorously decked out with a Latin ending, and the phrase seems to mean a 'gathering-place of all things.' *Omnibus* is a dative plural, 'for all,' and when we shorten it to *bus* we never think what a distance the Latin case ending has traveled when it has become, alone and unassisted, a name for a vehicle. The accusative is seen in *requiem* 'rest' and *vim* 'force,' and the ablative is found in *qua* 'where,' as when we say that Professor Hadzsits, *qua* editor, make certain recommendations — that is, he does so by virtue of his position as editor. *Rebus*, an expression of an idea 'by things' instead of by letters, is an ablative plural. *Via* 'by way of' is another ablative; so is *gratis* 'on account of thanks' and not because of money. Payment *in specie* 'in kind' has become *specie* payment with omission of the preposition. *Propaganda* is shortened from *de propaganda fide* 'about spreading the faith'; *manu-mit* 'to let go from the hand' and *loco-motive* 'moving from its place' have ablatives as their first parts. Several of our words are phrases composed of prepositions with ablatives: *extempore* is *ex tempore* 'according to the time,' *impromptu* is *in promptu* 'in readiness,' *subpena* is *sub poena* 'under penalty.'

Even a considerable number of verb forms have come into English as common words, the meanings of which in English are so familiar that we

give here only the meanings of the Latin words:
veto 'I forbid'; *ignoramus* 'we don't know';
tenet 'he holds'; *habitat* 'it dwells'; *affidavit* 'he
has sworn thereto'; *peccavi* 'I have sinned';
caret 'it is lacking'; *fiat* 'let it be done'; *im-
primatur* 'let it be printed'; *exit* 'he goes out';
exeunt 'they go out' — but the noun *exit* is from
Latin *exitus*. *Fascimile* contains the imperative
fac 'make'; *recipe* is an imperative, 'take';
query is slightly altered from the imperative *quaere* 'ask.' *Memento* also is an imperative, 'remember!' A number of Latin infini-
tives have come into English, somewhat changed,
but retaining the characteristic *r* of the ending:
such are *manor* from *manere* 'to remain,' *leisure*
from *licere* 'to be permitted,' *pleasure* from
placere 'to be pleasing,' *tender* 'to reach out'
from *tendere*, with the same meaning. *Render*
and its compound *surrender* are from *reddere*
'to give back,' with an *n* in imitation of its op-
posite *prendere* 'to seize.' *Power* is from *potere*
'to be able,' which in late Latin replaced the
classical *posse;* and *posse* itself denotes the
sheriff's means of pursuing and catching crim-
inals. *Behavior* is a mixture of the French form
of *habere* 'to have,' with the English verb *be-
have. Interest* is for *interesse* 'to be between,

difference,' with a final *t* in imitation of the word *debt*.

There are some other words, Latin words, which are used without change in English. Among these are *nil* 'nothing,' *extra* 'outside,' [30] *per* 'by,' *pro* 'on behalf of,' *versus* 'facing,' *bis* 'twice,' *interim* 'meanwhile,' *gradatim* 'step by step,' *seriatim* 'item by item,' *verbatim* 'word by word.' An *ante* is that which is put 'in front'; an *alias* is a name used 'at another time,' and an *alibi* is a proof that a person was 'at another place.' *Item* is the word 'likewise' prefixed to the next article in a list, especially in a bill, until it came to mean the article itself. *Quasi* 'as if' is prefixed to a word to indicate that its application is only seemingly valid, as when we speak of a *quasi-historical* event. *Tandem* denotes a style of harnessing horses 'at length' instead of side by side. But *con*, in the phrase *pro* and *con*, is only half of a Latin word, being shortened for *contra; sub* is shortened for *substitute*, and *super* for *supernumerary*, so that Latin cannot claim to have given these two prepositions to English as independent words.

These are but samples of the Latin forms which have come into English unchanged. There are whole groups of words, many of which have been touched upon in preceding chapters, that might be repeated here, as in the terminology of the sciences, and in the application of Latin suffixes. There are countless Latin phrases which are in familiar use, such as *sub rosa* and *sine die;* there are initial words such as *Paternoster* and *Magnificat,* used to denote the prayers, etc., of which they form the beginning. But we must not prolong the discussion *ad infinitum.* The unchanged Greek words must receive mention.

The words which have come from Greek into English without change, or with only the change which was imposed upon them by going into Latin, are fewer than those which have come from Latin, but they make an imposing list.[31] Foremost among them we find a great number of technical terms of rhetoric and grammar, such as *apostrophe, hyperbole, synecdoche, iambus, prooemium, zeugma.* This list alone illustrates all three Greek declensions, with some of the changes which these words underwent on passing into Latin. The rhetorical *hyperbole* shows the Greek ending of the nominative, and the mathematical *hyperbola* shows the same word in Latinized form; *dyspepsia* and *nausea* have the same ending in both languages. In the second declension, *discus* and *typhus* show the Latinized ending, while *asbestos* keeps the Greek form. *Asbestos* meant properly 'unquenched' or 'unquenchable,' [32] but is now applied to a material which cannot be set on fire. Among the neuters of the second declension, we find the Latinized *electrum*, denoting a natural alloy of gold and silver, and the pure Greek *electron*, by which our physicists now name the divisions of the once indivisible atom; one Greek word does double service in the sciences. *Emporium*, too, seems to have helped the newspaper reporter who coined the word *boozorium*, as he termed the places where prohibited beverages might be purchased.

Greek plurals assume Latin forms in English, if the Latin differs from the Greek. We have *amoeba amoebae*, *iambus iambi*, *phenomenon phenomena*, *sphinx sphinges*, *iris irides*. These are typical of other words also, but the foreign plurals of Greek words in English seem not to be so frequent as the foreign plurals of Latin words. Yet in words like *basis* and *thesis* the foreign plural is always used; here we find *bases* and *theses*. Another type which sometimes occurs in English is represented by *stigma* and *stigmata*, though this plural is usually reserved to denote the wounds of Christ, and *stigmas* is commonly used as the plural of other meanings. Naturally, very many Greek words have plurals with the English ending, and *sphinxes* is certainly more familiar than the *sphinges* given above; the dictionaries countenance both forms. But there are four troublesome Greek words: *ibis, Cyclops, octopus, proboscis;* what are their plurals? Shall we say *ibises, Cyclopses, octopuses, proboscises,* as though they were pure English, or *ibides, Cyclopes, octopodes, proboscides,* as though they were Greek (which they are)? The dictionaries give us permission to do either, or even to say *octopi* and *prosbosces,* as though they were Latin words with vowel stems instead of consonant stems. Somebody once wrote *ibes,* but this has not become current. One authority permits *Cyclops* as a plural, perhaps by the influence of a French singular *Cyclope.* Such uncertainty shows merely that these words are not enough used in the plural to have received a standard form, and most of us probably avoid them, even as we avoid saying two *forcepses* or *forcipes* or *forceps;* there is authority for every one, but every one is as unpleasant to the ear as the sight of one *forceps* in the dentist's hand is unpleasant to the eye. *Forceps* is a Latin word, not a Greek word.

There are a few other Greek words in English which should be noted. Certain names of letters are used as English words: *alpha* and *omega* denote the beginning and the ending, since they were the first and the last letters of the alphabet;[33] *pi* has a mathematical meaning; *delta* and *iota* are familiar English words, and *jot* is only a different development of *iota*. The plural *apocrypha* denotes those uncanonical books of the Old Testament which when printed are 'hidden' between the Old Testament and the New Testament; but originally the word meant that these books were 'hidden' away from use in public worship. The *antipodes* are the places 'against our feet.' *Bacteria* also are rarely spoken of in the singular except by the technical scientist, for a single *bacterium* is too small to interest the ordinary man; when bacteria annoy him, they do it wholesale. The vocative form *Jesu* is often used in English hymns, and the exclamation *eureka* means 'I have found.' The preposition *anti* 'against' has become an English word;[34] but the preposition *hypo* 'under,' when used as a complete word in English, is really an abbreviation of *hyposulphite*.

In the word *diapason*, we have a preposition with the genitive plural feminine of the adjective, meaning 'through all,' used as a short form of the phrase ἡ διὰ πασῶν τῶν χορδῶν ἁρμονία 'the concord through or across all the strings or notes.'

A very great number of our personal names also are of classical origin.[35] *Mark* and *Claire* are Latin, and *George* and *Helen* are Greek; but the words have been somewhat changed in transmission. Other names keep the original forms; *Marcus* and *Clara* are examples. Among such names used as given or baptismal names to-day, there are both Latin praenomina, such as *Marcus* and *Lucius*, and Latin family names, like *Aure ius* and *Julius;* there are also Latin cognomina, like *Felix* and *Rex*. Still others were not used as persons' names until after classical times, as for example *Amor* 'love,' and *Amandus* 'deserving to be loved.' Women's names derived from Latin are even more numerous than men's names: among them are *Aurora* 'dawn,' *Carmen* 'song,' *Miranda* 'deserving to be admired,' *Vera* 'true,' and *Portia*, late spelling for *Porcia*, which, by its obvious connection with *porcus*, indicated originally a 'pig-keeper.' Greek names still in use include not only *Hector*, *Aeneas*, and *Ulysses*, but even *Sparta*, and Greek names for women include *Agatha* 'good,' *Alethea* 'truth,' *Sophia* 'wisdom,' *Zoe* 'life,' and *Zeta*, which is the name of a letter of the alphabet.

Mythological and historical personages of antiquity bequeathed to us their names in another value, as types of qualities. A man is said to be as imposing as *Jove*, or as handsome as *Apollo*, and a woman may be as queenly as *Juno*, or as lovely as *Venus*. The old legends, especially those connected with the city of Troy, are rich in such products: we speak of a *stentorian* voice from the strong-voiced Stentor mentioned once in the *Iliad*,[36] and of a *mentor* because that was the name assumed by the disguised Athena when she guided and counseled the youthful Telemachus in the *Odyssey;* we say as strong as *Hercules*, as fleet as *Achilles*, as enduring or as crafty as *Ulysses*, as lying as *Sinon*, as ill-starred as *Priam*, as stalwart as *Hector*, as beautiful as *Helen*, as faithful as *Penelope*. *Ajax defying the lightning* is a literary commonplace familiar to many who have not the faintest idea of the story which gives us the phrase. From historical times, *Leonidas* is a type of bravery, *Solon* is a typical law-giver,

Socrates is a synonym for a man of wisdom, the Lydian *Croesus* and the Roman *Crassus* suggest riches, *Demosthenes* and *Cicero* stand for eloquence, *Caesar* is a type of imperial power.

Literary personifications of inanimate objects show in English a strong classical influence. The sun is *he* and the moon is *she*, because Latin *sol* was masculine and Latin *luna* was feminine; but Anglo-Saxon *sunne* was feminine and *mona* was masculine. We always speak of a ship as *she*, because of the Latin feminine *navis*, though Anglo-Saxon *scipu* is a neuter word. We can repeat for English personifications the rule of Latin genders, that names of rivers, winds, months, and mountains are masculine; for the Mississippi overflows *his* banks, the North Wind freezes *his* victims, December brings *his* snow, Mt. Everest lures on the intrepid climbers who would stand upon *his* highest peak. *Death* alone, or almost alone, resists the Latin and keeps *his* native masculinity, in defiance of the feminine *mors*. Naturally, we find words where no conflict of the sexes takes place: winter is *he* and earth is *she*, in both the languages. But where there is a disagreement, it is almost always the Latin which determines the sex of the personified thing or idea, in English speech.

[125]

In general, the words which English has borrowed unchanged even to their endings, are pronounced in English with the accent on the syllable on which it falls in Latin, as in *aréna* and
nébula. Even Greek words conform to the
Latin accent in English, as in *asbéstos*, and *cha-
méleon*, which in Greek had the accents on the *as*
and the *le* respectively. To this principle there
are a few exceptions, especially in the longer
words in *átor*, which tend to get a new principal
accent two syllables earlier, and to reduce the
Latin accent to a secondary value: *législator*,
líberator, *véntilator*. In some others, the Latin
accent has been carried back from the penult
to the antepenult, as in *aúditor*, *compétitor*, *exéc-
utor*, *órator*, *sénator*. This is due to the general
tendency of English to draw the accent toward
the beginning of words; and the same shift of
the accent from its Latin position on the penult,
to the preceding syllable in English, is seen in
apothéosis, *cícatrix*, *metamórphosis*, *óctopus*, *ór-
chestra*, *sínister*, where the lexicographers still
recognize also the pronunciation with the accent
on the penult as in Latin, although in most instances they prefer the accent on the antepenult.
On the other hand, *arbútus* and *gladiólus* are
more commonly used than Latin *árbutus* and

gladíolus, which is contrary to the English tendency to shift the accent toward the beginning of the word; we seem here to have 'leaned backward' in trying to accent the words properly, and to have failed in the attempt.

From these examples, which are only selections, we see that Latin and Greek have given us a great number of words which retain even their endings, that of the nominative singular in most instances, but also many plural forms of the nominative, and a sprinkling of other case forms, of verb forms, and of adverbs and prepositions. Many of these words are in use as personal names; and other names are familiar in literature and even in ordinary conversation as outstanding instances of virtues or of vices. A reasonable appreciation of these words and forms can hardly be had without some knowledge of the languages from which they sprang; and thus, from another side, an understanding of Latin and Greek is valuable for our use of our own language.

XI. GRAMMATICAL STUDIES

OUR own way of viewing grammar may be traced back to the Greeks. If we pass over some earlier efforts in this field, for the true beginning of systematic grammatical studies we must look to Dionysius Thrax, who lived in the first half of the second century B.C. Dionysius was one of the most important pupils of the famous literary critic Aristarchus, at Alexandria in Egypt. He composed the first formal grammar which has come down to us; he conceived the subject, however, in a wide sense, dividing it into six parts: reading to music, exposition of texts, repetition of words and stories, etymology, paradigms, literary criticism. He treats the accent, the marks of punctuation, the various letters, which he distinguishes as vowels and consonants; then the syllables, classified as short, long, and common. He defines the word and the sentence, and enumerates and explains the eight parts of speech: noun, verb, participle, article, pronoun, preposition, adverb, conjunction — differing little from our present list. He discusses also the declensions and the conjugations, but does not deal with syntax and style.

At Rome, the first definite interest in grammar was created by Crates of Mallos, who came to Rome about 169 B.C., as ambassador of Attalus, King of Pergamus. During his stay, Crates lectured to many gatherings; and other visiting Greeks and certain Romans followed his example. Their lectures and writings were chiefly expositions of texts, explaining difficult words and forms. But a different type of grammatical treatise, more like that of Dionysius Thrax, also came into existence; the first of these of which we have extensive portions extant is the *De Lingua Latina* of Marcus Terentius Varro (116–27 B.C.), in twenty-five books: I, introduction; II–VII, etymology of words; VIII–XIII, forms of the declensions and conjugations; XIV–XXV, syntax. We still have V–X, except for a few lost sections.

In later times there were many school grammars, most of them largely copied from predecessors in the field.[37] The most important of these, from the standpoint of later influence, was the *Ars grammatica* of Aelius Donatus, who wrote at Rome in the middle of the fourth century; it is extant in two versions, a shorter form and a longer form. The shorter form discusses concisely, by the method of question and answer, the eight parts of speech: noun, pronoun, verb, adverb, participle, conjunction, preposition, interjection. The longer form takes up successively sounds, letters, syllables, metrical feet, accents, punctuation marks, the parts of speech, barbarisms, solecisms, and other errors, poetical licenses in forms and in syntax, and figures of rhetoric. Donatus's grammar was much used in later centuries, and the author's name gave to French and to English the word *donat* or *donet*, which, though at first indicating only his own grammar, came to mean any introductory Latin grammar, and finally an elementary treatise on any subject. The employment of this word in English literature of the fourteenth to the sixteenth centuries testifies eloquently to the influence of Donatus upon the study of Latin and of grammar in general during that period.

But the formal study of the English language was late in starting; for Latin and French, as the languages of government and of polite society, were worthy objects of study rather than the popular dialect which the child learned by absorption. The first extant grammar of the Latin language written in English is that by William Lily, printed in 1527, with an introduction by John Colet.[38] It contains an account of the letters of the alphabet, Greek as well as Latin, followed by sections on the number and declension of nouns, adjectives and their comparison, and pronouns; the paradigms of verbs, both regular and irregular, with participles, supines, and gerundives; and finally the adverbs, conjunctions, prepositions, and interjections. The remainder is a method for turning English sentences into Latin, and necessarily deals with syntax, though not in a systematic way; but in the edition of 1566, the second part is devoted to the principles of syntax.

Lily's grammar has an especial interest for us, because it was studied in school by the greatest of all English poets, William Shakespeare; that it was used by him is quite natural, for King Henry VIII, according to the title-page of the 1542 edition, had granted the book an exclusive right to publication for school use. This monopoly was apparently never formally revoked, although other grammars of Latin were in use in the seventeenth century; but many of them were only slight modifications of Lily's, and Lily's rules of syntax were well known until the early nineteenth century. Lily's work is important for English grammar, since it set a standard of arrangement of the material, in that a Latin paradigm with English translation alongside easily suggested that English forms be presented in similar tabulations, with the same terminology as for Latin. In at least one instance this produced an illogical naming of the forms; for Greek and Latin say *I and you and he came*, which gives the terms *first, second, third persons*, but English is required by politeness to say *you and he and I came*, so that the first person is third in order, the second is first, and the third is second. Yet we retain the classical terms for the different persons, without any protest.

A method like Lily's will teach not only Latin, but also English, since the instruction is given in English; and while this may have delayed the composition of specifically English grammars, it also paved the way for their appearance. Accordingly, within the century after the appearance of Lily's grammar, we find several grammars of English.[39] In 1568, Thomas Smith published at Paris a work called *De recta et emendata linguae Anglicae scriptione dialogus*, in Latin, which treated only the letters and their sounds, with the English words in a phonetic alphabet. In 1580, James Bellot published at London *Le maistre d'escole anglais or The Englishe Scholemaister*, a method by which speakers of French might acquire a correct pronunciation of English; in parallel columns of French and English he discussed letters, pronunciation, articles, pronouns, verb forms, and the distinction of homonyms. In 1586, William Bullokar published *A Bref Grammar for English;* he wrote also a *Booke at Large for the Amendment of Orthographie for English Speech*. There are English grammars by John Stockwood in 1590, by Alexander Gill in 1621, and by John Hewes in 1624. In 1622, George Mason published a *Grammaire anglaise*, in French, a method-book for speakers of French to learn English; it treats the pronunciation, certain words and suffixes, declensions of nouns, conjugation of verbs, and some idiomatic phrases. Charles Butler's *English Grammar*, printed in a phonetic alphabet at Oxford, in 1634, treats the letters and their sounds, syllables, the formation of the plural and of the genitive of nouns, the comparison and composition of adjectives, the declension and use of pronouns, the forms of verbs, prepositions, adverbs, and punctuation, and it ends with an index and explanation of homonyms. In 1640, Simon Daines issued his *Orthoepia Anglicana*, which treats the letters and their sounds, rules of spelling, the use of punctuation marks, and the writing of correspondence.

We come now to a more important work, *The English Grammar, made by Ben Jonson, for the benefit of all strangers, out of his observation of the English language, now spoken and in use,* printed at London in 1640. This is a first draft, published three years after its author's death; the finished manuscript was destroyed by a fire in his study, about 1629. The first part deals with etymology, in twenty-two chapters, the headings of which indicate their contents: *Of Grammar and the Parts, Of Letters and their Powers, Of the Vowels, Consonants, Dipthongs, Syllabes* (which is the older spelling), *Accent, Notation of a Word, Parts of Speech, Nouns, Diminution of Nouns, Comparisons, First Declension, Second Declension, Pronouns, Verb, First Conjugation, Second Conjugation, Third Conjugation, Fourth Conjugation, Adverbs, Conjunctions.* The second part is on syntax, in nine chapters : *Of Apostrophus, Of the Syntax of One Noun with Another, Of the Syntax of a Pronoun with a Noun, of Adjectives, of a Verb with a Noun, of a Verb with a Verb, of Adverbs, of Conjunctions, Of the Distinction of Sentences.*

Jonson, in the title of his work, professed to have composed it "out of his own observation of the English language;" but an examination shows many more features of indebtedness to the classical models than of independence from them. The arrangement of the material is strikingly like that in the work of Donatus, and still more like that of some of the longer and more detailed works of the Latin grammarians ; for example, a whole chapter is devoted to the formation of diminutives of nouns, which is quite important in Latin, but is of very little consequence in English. Jonson recognized the same parts of speech as in Latin, still including both substantive and adjective under the term *noun.* He kept the participle as a separate part of speech, and counted the articles among the pronouns. This last grouping, though surprising to us to-day, was not unnatural, for Latin *unus* and *ille*, which were often pronouns, developed into the articles of late Latin and of French, and a precisely similar relation might be assumed to exist in English: as it happens, *a* and *the* have in fact come from Anglo-Saxon words meaning *one* and *that*, even as the French articles have come from Latin words meaning *one* and *that*. Jonson counted two declensions of nouns in English, distinguished by the manner of forming the plural: the first declension added *s* or *es*, the second added *en*. He explained *men* and *women* as contractions for *manen* and *womanen*, and failed to mention *feet*, *geese*, *lice*, *mice*, and *deer*, *sheep*. He recognized six genders of nouns: the usual *masculine*, *feminine*, and *neuter*, and *epicene* (in words properly denoting male beings or female beings only, but used for both sexes), *doubtful* (in nouns denoting beings of both sexes), *common of three* (such as adjectives, which denote all three genders without change in English). In this, he was merely following the current Latin classification of his time. He was influenced by Latin also when in English he counted stars, months, and winds as masculine, and islands, countries, and cities as feminine; for while some of these often have such values by the principle of personification, they cannot be said normally to be personified in English. He divided English verbs into four conjugations, precisely as in Latin; the first

[136]

forms the past and the participle with *d* or *t*, the fourth has the *d* or *t* and also a vowel change, the second and the third have a vowel change without the added *d* or *t*. But the reader cannot find Jonson's criterion for distinguishing the second and the third. On the other hand, by studying from the English standpoint to the neglect of the Latin phenomena, Jonson failed utterly to recognize the true subjunctive form in English, in such a sentence as *It is preposterous to execute a man, before he have been condemned;* but thinking that *have* was here a plural form, he stated that singular nouns often take plural verbs, "especially when the verb is joined to an adverb or conjunction." Even in this connection, he cited similar lack of agreement in Latin, as in Ovid's *Omnia pontus erat,* although the only common feature is that in some combinations the subject and the verb do not agree in number. Thus, throughout the work, Jonson betrays his dependence on Latin studies and methods; indeed, the opening chapters on the letters and the sounds are accompanied by copious parallel passages from Roman grammarians, cited in Latin.

But sufficient has been said to show the dependence of the manner of presentation of English grammar, upon that of Latin, which in turn got its impulse and its form from Greek. Later works on the grammar of English show merely a more skillful adaptation of the old method, to the English subject matter, which differs from Latin chiefly in having fewer forms of the declensions and conjugations, and in making greater use of other means to show the relations of the words to one another; for English uses more prepositions and more auxiliary verbs than Latin does, and employs the order of the words to show their relations, while Latin uses word-order chiefly to indicate the relative emphasis of the words.

Notwithstanding these differences between Latin and modern English, the oldest form of English, namely Anglo-Saxon, was a highly inflected language very similar to Latin in forms and in syntax; and the essentials of case in nouns, of person and number in verbs, of the use of the subjunctive mood, and of the various agreements between different members of the sentence, still abide in English, and are rarely well understood except by those who know them in their Latin aspect.[40]

XII. GRAMMATICAL TERMINOLOGY

AS has been mentioned, our grammatical terminology is almost entirely taken from Latin; and the Romans, when they began to study formal grammar, had to transliterate or to translate the terms from Greek, where the terminology had already been developed. The Romans added a few words for grammatical categories which did not exist in Greek. This is clear from the following list of equivalent terms:

(τέχνη) γραμματική	(ars) grammatica	grammar
τὸ γράμμα	littera	letter
τὰ σύμφωνα	consonantes	consonants
τὰ φωνήεντα	vocales	vowels
ἡ δίφθογγος	diphthongus	diphthong
ἡ προσῳδία	accentus	accent
ὀξεῖα	acutus	acute
βαρεῖα	gravis	grave
περισπωμένη	circumflexus	circumflex
ἡ ἐτυμολογία	etymologia	etymology
τὸ παράδειγμα	paradigma	paradigm
ἡ κλίσις	declinatio	declension
ἡ συζυγία	conjugatio	conjugation
ἡ σύνταξις	syntaxis	syntax
	constructio	construction
τὰ μέρη τὰ τῆς φωνῆς	partes orationis	parts of speech

τὸ ὄνομα	nomen	noun
οὐσιαστικόν	substantivum	substantive
ἐπίθετον	adjectivum	adjective
ἡ πτῶσις	casus	case
ὀνομαστική	nominativus	nominative
γενική	genetivus	genitive
δοτική	dativus	dative
αἰτιατική	accusativus	accusative
κλητική	vocativus	vocative
	ablativus	ablative
	locativus	locative
ὁ ἀριθμός	numerus	number
ἐνικός	singularis	singular
δυικός	dualis	dual
πληθυντικός	pluralis	plural
τὸ γένος	genus	gender
ἀρσενικόν	masculinum	masculine
θηλυκόν	femininum	feminine
οὐδέτερον	neutrum	neuter
ἐπίκοινον	epicoenum	epicene
ἡ παράθεσις	comparatio	comparison
ὁ βαθμός	gradus	grade, degree
θετικός	positivus	positive
συγκριτικός	comparativus	comparative
ὑπερθετικός	superlativus	superlative
ἡ ἀντωνυμία	pronomen	pronoun
τὸ ἄρθρον	articulus	article
τὸ ῥῆμα	verbum	verb
ἐνεργητικόν	activum	active
μέσον	medium	middle
παθητικόν	passivum	passive
ἡ ἔγκλισις	modus	mode, mood
ὁριστική	indicativus	indicative
προστακτική	imperativus	imperative
ὑποτακτική	subjunctivus	subjunctive

εὐκτική	optativus	optative
ἀπαρέμφατος	infinitivus	infinitive
μετοχή	participium	participle
	gerundivum	gerundive
	gerundium	gerund
	supinum	supine
ὁ χρόνος	tempus	tense
ἐνεστώς	praesens	present
παρατατικός	imperfectum	imperfect
μέλλων	futurum	future
παρακείμενος	perfectum	perfect
ὑπερσυντελικός	plusquamperfectum	pluperfect
τὸ πρόσωπον	persona	person
πρῶτον	prima	first
τὸ ἐπίρρημα	adverbium	adverb
ἡ πρόθεσις	praepositio	preposition
ὁ σύνδεσμος	conjunctio	conjunction
τὸ ἐπιφώνημα	interjectio	interjection

A glance at the list shows clearly, even to one who knows no Latin, that the English terms are practically all taken from Latin. Of those given in the list, only *speech, middle, mood, first* are native English, and one of these, *mood*, is a confusion of the native word with the synonymous *mode*. The way in which the terms got their applications, is however not always apparent. Let us interpret some of them. A *noun* is a name, *nomen*, and originally included the adjective as well as that which we commonly term the noun; in technical writing, it often has the inclusive meaning even to-day. As the name of an actual thing having existence or substance, the noun is a *substantive;* as the name of a quality or attribute, which has no existence by itself, but is 'placed on' the substantive, the noun is called an *adjective*. The declension was graphically represented as a quadrant, the upper right-hand sector of a circle, with several radii representing the cases. The vertical radius was the *casus rectus* or *straight case*, and the others were *casus obliqui* or *oblique cases*, because they were 'slanting.' The *declension*, recited from the nominative as a start, became therefore a 'bending or leaning downward,' and every *casus* was a 'fall' from the previous position; that is, every one represented a 'fall' except the first or 'straight case,' which took the name *case* from the others.

Sometimes the Romans mistranslated the Greek terms. *Accusative* is a wrong interpretation of a Greek word meaning 'pertaining to the thing affected,' not badly represented by the modern term *objective*. *Genitive* 'pertaining to the source' is wrongly rendered for 'pertaining to the genus, generic'; but the use of this case to denote the name of the father, as in *Marci filius*, seems to have influenced the choice of the Latin term. *Possessive*, used later as a synonym for *genitive*, is a more logical term, but is not a translation of the Greek. The *participle* is a 'partaker, sharer,' since it partakes of the natures both of the adjective and of the verb; it has declension like the adjective, and governs objects like the verb. A *letter* is a 'scratch,' which suggests the nature of the first writing; the English word *write* also means 'scratch.' A *syllable* is a 'taking together' of certain sounds which are pronounced as a unit. A *consonant* is that which 'sounds with' a vowel, since it is not pronounced alone in any word. A *diphthong* is that which contains 'two sounds.' An *article* is a 'joint' or 'link.' An *infinitive* is 'not limited' as to person and number. And so on; for in this manner all the grammatical terms may be explained.

The important fact for our purpose is that native English has contributed practically nothing to the English terminology of grammar, and that Greek, either by translation into Latin, or by mere transliteration, has furnished practically everything.

XIII. THE ALPHABET AND WRITING

OUR alphabet is readily traced back to the Greeks; and the Greeks had a very persistent tradition that the knowledge of letters came to them from the Phoenicians. The belief was formerly held that the Phoenicians got writing from the Egyptians; but this theory is somewhat discredited to-day. The discovery of very ancient writing in Crete has given us the theory that the Greeks received their letters from the Cretans, either directly or through the Phoenicians, or possibly through the Hittites, another people of Asia Minor; but this cannot be considered proven. The close resemblance of the Greek names of the letters to the names of the letters in Hebrew, a dialect very like Phoenician, would seem to establish the correctness of the belief of the Greeks that they derived writing from the Phoenicians; thus the first four letters of the alphabet are in Hebrew called *'Aleph, Beth, Gimel, Daleth*, and in Greek *Alpha, Beta, Gamma, Delta*.

Now the alphabet which the Greeks used in their various cities was not everywhere uniform;

the signs varied in form, the letters varied in order, certain symbols varied in value. The alphabet which came into general use among the Greeks, and is still used, was that of the Ionic cities of Asia Minor; that which was the source of the Latin alphabet, was the alphabet used at Cumae, a city near Naples in Italy, founded by colonists from Chalcis in Euboea, who brought with them their local alphabet. The Cumaean letters are well known to us from ancient inscriptions; and for ease of comparison we give the Ionic alphabet, the Cumaean alphabet in slightly normalized form, and the Latin equivalents:

	1	2	3	4	5	6	7	8	9	10	11	12	13	14
Ionic	A	B	Γ	Δ	E		Z	H	Θ	I	K	Λ	M	N
Cumaean	A	B	C	D	E	F	Z	H	Θ		I	K	L	M	N
Latin	A	B	C	D	E	F		G	H		I	K	L	M	N

	15	16	17	18	19	20	21	22	23	24	25	26	27	28
Ionic	Ξ	O	Π				P	Ϟ	T	Y		Φ	X	Ψ	Ω
Cumaean	⊞	O	P	M	Ϙ	R	S	T	V	X	Φ	↓		
Latin		O	P			Q	R	S	T	V	X			

Where the Latin alphabet, which we still use, differs from the Greek, we find that it is because the Cumaean alphabet differed from the Ionic Greek, as in Nos. 3, 4, 12, 17, 20, 21, 23. No. 3 had in Greek the value *g*, and so also in some early Latin inscriptions; but the Romans ceased

to write K in most words, and represented its
sound also by C. Presently, to avoid the confusion, they took a variant form of Z (for which
at the time they had no need), or else a C with a
diacritical mark, to represent *g*, and put it in
the old place of Z; but C for *g* always survived
in *C.* and *Cn.*, the abbreviations for *Gaius* and
Gnaeus — the Romans had no names *Caius* and
Cnaeus. F, called *digamma*, had in Greek the
sound of English *w*, and was used in Latin for
the similar sound of *f*. H, named *hēta*, was in
Ionic a long *e*, for the Ionians had lost the sound
h, and *hēta* was to them merely *ēta;* but the
Cumaeans kept their *h*'s, and therefore H is *h*
in Latin. A form of M with five strokes is
responsible for *M'.*, the abbreviation for *Manius*,
the apostrophe being a remnant of the fifth
stroke; *M.* stands for *Marcus*. The Cumaean
S was a three-stroke form, either angular or
curved; the Ionic form is an angular one of
four strokes. Nos. 15 and 18, though written
in the alphabet of Cumae, were obsolete, since
their values were given also by Nos. 24 and 21
respectively. Ionic Ⲭ and Cumaean X had the
same value, *x*, while Ionic X meant χ or *ch;*
Cumaean represented χ by ↓, which in Ionic
meant ψ or *ps*. Cumaean had no special char-

[146]

acters for *ps*, nor for the long *e* and *o*, which Ionic represented by H and Ω. Some of these last variations are due to the fact that the Phoenician alphabet had but twenty-two letters, and therefore all Greek letters after No. 22 are special Greek additions, differing in different localities.

Nos. 9, 25, 26, the Greek *θ*, *φ*, *χ*, were somewhat like *th* in *hothouse*, *ph* in *uphill*, *kh* in *blockhouse;* and as these sounds did not occur in Latin, the letters were utilized as numerals. Θ denoted 100; after a time, the interior dot was omitted, and the right side was opened, as though it were the initial of *centum*. Φ, with the vertical not extending beyond the circle, was 1000; in a running hand, with an opening at the bottom and two curves at the top, it was easily transformed into M, as though the initial of *mille*. D, for 500, is the right half of the circular Φ. No. 26 of the Cumaean letters meant 50; the side strokes were lowered to the horizontal, and the left stroke then omitted, so that it became identical with L. Thus of the four numerals, not one is the letter which it seems to be. Of the others, I is a single stroke to denote 1; V is a conventionalized hand outline, one stroke portraying the thumb and the

other stroke the four fingers, and meant 5 ; X
is two hand outlines united at the wrist, and
meant 10.

Thus the Romans secured an alphabet of
twenty-one letters, A B C D E F G H I K L M N
O P Q R S T V X. But in the days of
Greek literary influence, they found that they
needed means of representing two other Greek
letters in borrowed words: Greek Y (now
printed Υ), sounded like French *u*, and Greek
Z, sounded like English *z*. The Romans, lacking these sounds in native words, but needing
means of writing them in words taken from
Greek, transferred Y and Z bodily from the
Greek alphabet, and placed them at the end of
their own alphabet ; this was done in the first
century B.C.

J, U, and W remain to be explained. I represented both the vowel *i* and the consonant *y* ;
an ornamental form with a tail was sometimes
employed in headings and at the end of words.
In the Middle Ages, this tailed form was specialized for the consonant, our J ; but it is still
used at the end of words and of numerals in
medical prescriptions, as in *sodij brom. gtt. viij
(saturated solution)*, for eight drops of a saturated
solution of sodium bromide. Similarly, V rep-

resented both vowel *u* and consonant *w*; Latin did not then have the sound of English *v*. U was merely a running-hand form of V; in later times, U was specialized as the vowel and V as the consonant. When this took place, Latin V had shifted its sound to that of English *v*; but the Germanic languages had a native sound *w*, and to express it as distinct from the *v*, they wrote the V twice, whence W is called *double u*.

The names of the letters are not without interest. If we allow for change of pronunciation in the transfer from Latin to English, the names which we now use seem to have been current in ancient Italy, though they were not borrowed from the Greeks, except in the case of Z. The vowels had the names of their sounds: *a e i o u wi*. The last is for *ui*, an early Roman attempt to represent the sound of the Greek letter, which was like French *u*; in *ui* the first part was a vowel, but it later became a consonant. The consonants had the names of their sounds, supported by the vowel *e*; *be ce de ge pe te ve ze, ef el em en es ex*; *er*, which in English become *ar* by the influence of the *r*, as in the British pronunciation of *clerk*. *Ce ka qu* have different vowels to give the three Latin K-sounds, automatically, certain slight differences, which, if not detected by ear, can be felt in the shift of the contact of the tongue with the palate as they are pronounced in *ken, can, cup*. *Ja* has *a* to rhyme with *ka*. *Ache* seems to be a strengthening of *h* in *ahe*, as in the medieval *michi* and *nichil* for *mihi* and *nihil*. Z is called not only *ze*, but *zed*, from Greek *zeta*, and *izzard*, a corruption of French *et zède* ' and z.' The character &, sometimes set at the end of the English alphabet, is a manuscript form of Latin *et* ' and,' and is called *and*, or occasionally *ampersand* ' and, per se and,' and in Scotch *epershand* ' et, per se and.'

In explaining the new letters J, U, and W, we anticipated a little. When the Romans conquered Britain in the first century after Christ, they brought with them their system of writing; and though Roman learning must have suffered an eclipse after the final withdrawal of the Romans in 402, it was revived by the efforts of the Christian missionaries. For the missionaries, carrying with them their sacred books, were everywhere ministers not of religion only, but of learning and of education; and by them the Latin alphabet again gained currency in the island.

But the alphabet which has so far been de-

[150]

scribed, consists of capital letters only; the differences between capitals and small letters, between print and script, and the like, remain to be explained, and this is no easy task, without illustrative plates. Yet an attempt must be made in simple form and in few words.

Writing on stone or metal, by chiseling or engraving the letters, is naturally done in straight lines, unless the forms of the letters, as of C, D, O, etc., require curves; such letters are known as Square Capitals, and the style of writing is called the Monumental Style. In scratching wax with a stilus or in using pen and ink on paper or parchment, ease promotes the use of curved lines and the development of a running hand, known as Cursive Writing. These two styles, fundamentally alike yet apparently very different, were in use among the Romans, and were not infrequently employed on materials inappropriate to them; as when a carefully written manuscript was executed in the Square Capitals. But in manuscripts, the capitals were often modified, so as to have shorter and less regular horizontal strokes, with serifs ornamenting the ends of the verticals, as in our normal typography to-day; these were called, without special fitness, Rustic Capitals. From the capitals came another

[151]

development in rounded forms, the Uncial, or 'inch-high' — a misleading name, since these letters were rarely so high; this style was common in the fourth century. Further development of the uncial, with some influence from the cursive, gave the Half-uncial or Minuscule, which is really responsible for the small letters as compared with the capitals; the earliest examples are in the sixth century. After this, writing split into national hands, Lombardic in Italy, Visigothic in Spain, Merovingian in the Frankish Empire; each had two styles, a truly cursive form, and a book-hand, employed for more formal purposes by professional scribes, with a certain admixture of uncial and half-uncial forms. About 800, the Caroline Minuscule developed from the Merovingian, and presently spread all over the continent, superseding the older national hands, but itself acquiring variations and degenerating in the different countries. It was again reformed in the time of the Renaissance.

Missionaries had long since introduced a half-uncial style into Ireland, where it developed into a special Irish script; this the monks carried into the north of England. Various styles of writing which Roman missionaries brought into the south of England, seem never to have become thoroughly naturalized; but with the Norman Conquest there came a Caroline script of a predominantly cursive nature, which was used for all official documents. This produced on English soil two styles, a Court hand and a Chancery hand. The Court hand was characterized by a lateral compression which cramps and narrows the letters, and was used until the reign of George II; the Chancery hand was marked by a fanciful angular and upright treatment of the letters, and is still in use as an engrossing style for enrollments and patents. But the native hand had persisted for Anglo-Saxon writings and for an occasional official charter issued in the language of the people; with certain modifications from the official Caroline script, it gave an English book-hand, the origin of our " Old English " style of printing. Our present-day handwriting and its printed equivalent, italics, came from Italy in the time of the Renaissance, the beauty and clearness of the style giving it a manifest superiority and promoting its spread.

On English soil, however, a few special characters were used which should be noted. From Ireland came a flat-headed g, looking like a figure 3 or a script z, whose proper sound was that of *y*; because of its appearance, it was changed to *z* in a few personal names, as in *Menzies, Dalziel, Cadzow, Mackenzie*, in some of which it is now also sounded as a *z*, instead of as *y*. Another special character in the Anglo-Saxon handwriting, of Roman origin, is a crossed *d*, *ð*, with the value of *th* in *the;* it is used interchangeably with *þ*, named *thorn*, whose proper sound is that of *th* as in *thorn*, though it is used also for *th* as in *the*, which is then printed *ye*. Such a *ye* is none the less to be read *the*. This character *thorn* comes from the old system of writing called the Runes, which developed in northern Europe either from Roman writing or, possibly, from Greek writing at an earlier date, as brought by traders; the forms of the letters were apparently modified by the use of wood or bark as writing material, where the cutter can easily cut strokes toward himself, while strokes away from himself are almost impossible. In *viz.*, an abbreviation for *videlicet* ' it is permissible to see,' the last character is not a *z*, but an old manuscript sign of abbreviation, used in many countries; we read it *namely*, not *viz*.

Thus our capital letters, with and without serifs, our small letters, our script and our italics, our Old English print, and all our other styles of writing and printing are directly developed from the writing of the Romans, who themselves owe the alphabet to the Greeks. What an incalculably precious gift they have bestowed upon us!

XIV. CONCLUSION : LATINLESS ENGLISH

WE have seen the occasions on which the English language borrowed from Latin and from Greek. We have found that English owes to the classical languages about two thirds of its vocabulary, that is, of the different words, and about one sixth to one third of all words used, without excluding repetitions ; that many monosyllabic words, and practically the entire technical terminology of the arts and sciences, come from the classics ; that the means used to-day for making new words, namely the prefixes and the suffixes, are those coming from Latin and Greek, almost to the exclusion of Anglo-Saxon prefixes and suffixes ; that even many Latin and Greek forms are used unchanged as English words. Our manner of presenting grammatical studies, our alphabet, and our different styles of printing and of writing — these too we owe to the Greeks and Romans.

So much we have seen ; and after all, what would English be without Latin and Greek?

Let us take a few specimens of English with blank spaces representing the words or parts of words, which we have received from the classics :

"When in the —— of —— ——s, it becomes —— for one —— to —— the —— bands which have ——ed them with another, and to —— among the ——s of the earth, the —— and —— —— to which the Laws of —— and of ——'s God —— them, a —— —— to the ——s of mankind ——s that they should —— the ——s which —— them to the ——."

Probably this will be recognized as the opening sentence of the American Declaration of Independence.[41] Let us try another selection in the same way :

"In —— to —— —— —— and to —— —— —— and —— by the —— of —— not to —— to war, by the —— of open, —— and —— ——s between ——s, by the —— —— of the understandings of —— law as the —— —— of —— among ——s, and by the —— of —— and a —— —— for all —— ——s in the dealings of ——ed ——s with one another, the High ——ing ——es —— to this —— of the —— of ——s."

This is less familiar, and we should perhaps need to be told that it is the preamble to the

Covenant of the League of Nations. And now a third and final extract, similarly delatinized :

" In the —— of a —— dead in this ——, —— always has, does, will, must take —— over ——, and the choice between a dead and living —— as an —— of —— has many —— ——es which it would be ——ing to —— out in ——, with the —— whether a —— of —— would learn most of life by —— ing —— or giving his —— to the —— and —— of to-day. Happily for ——, ——s in ——s have been very —— and —— in their ——s and more mindful of the whole —— field than are the ——s for the —— of —— - —— ——ly ; for their —— of —— —— - —— has under ——d ——s become a —— ——."

Without the words of classical origin, we can get practically no idea what the writer is trying to say ; we can still observe, however, several errors in his use of English. It chances that this passage is a particularly savage attack on the study of Latin and Greek, by G. Stanley Hall.[42]

These three passages illustrate the debt of the English language to the languages of Greece and Rome, more eloquently and convincingly, than many pages of statistics and of linguistic history.

NOTES AND BIBLIOGRAPHY

NOTES

1. The figures are cited also in *The Classical Weekly*, VII. 137–138 (1913). There is a valuable article on this subject, by B. L. Ullman, in *The Classical Journal*, XVIII. 82–90 (1922).

2. Cf. G. M. Wilson and K. J. Hoke, *How to Measure*, New York, 1920, chapter II, especially pp. 6–7.

3. Greek verse was read in virtually all lands, but Latin verse was read only where Latin was the vernacular. So said Cicero, in his oration *Pro Archia Poeta*, § 23.

4. For clearness and convenience, English words are in this book usually cited in the modern form, rather than in the older form which they had at the time under discussion.

5. Bradley, *The Making of English*, 81, adds the following to the list of words taken from Latin by the Anglo-Saxons while they were still on the continent: *street, mile, wine, butter, pepper, cheese, silk, alum, pound, inch.*

6. Perhaps *down* was borrowed by the Anglo-Saxons while still on the continent; *bin*, meaning 'manger' originally, and *dun*, the name of a color, seem to be the only certain early borrowings of English from the Celtic of the island; cf. Bradley, *The Making of English*, 82–83.

7. But *street* and *mile* may have been borrowed by the Anglo-Saxons before they crossed to the island; cf. Note 5.

8. *Angel, verse*, and a few others have been remade in English at a later date so as to resemble their Latin originals more closely.

9. *Ass* is certainly not Latin by origin; but the source from which it came into Latin is doubtful. *Fiddle, cope, nun*

may be borrowings of Latin from some other tongue which cannot now be determined.

10. For our purposes, it is unnecessary to distinguish the older English dialects and their separate influences on modern English.

11. For convenience, the term *classical* is, from this point onward, freely used to mean *of Latin or Greek origin,* in speaking of English words or parts of English words. By *classical Latin,* however, we mean Latin before about 200 A.D., while *late Latin* applies to Latin of a time too recent for its new words to be placed in our usual Latin dictionaries.

12. One Latin word, giving 5 entries and 18 occurrences, has been excluded as not certainly the source of the Anglo-Saxon words.

13. In some instances, the English word comes from a derivative of the word quoted, and not from it directly.

14. Such interpretations are intended to give the original meanings of the words, and not their present significance, which is often materially changed from the original meaning.

15. In the following lists, words after the + sign have no Latin or Greek originals old enough to be found in our usual Latin and Greek dictionaries, but were composed at a later date; those after the dash are hybrids of English and the classics. Statement is made also whether the prefix is *inseparable* (never used as a separate word), *prepositional* (capable of use as a preposition), or *adverbial* (an adverb when used separately, and never a preposition).

Prefixes of Latin origin, found in English words:

Ab 'away, from,' prep.: *aberrant, ablution, absolute, abs-cess, abs-cond, abs-temious, a-vert, a-mentia, ap-erient* + *ab-judge.*
Ad 'to, in addition to,' prep.: *adapt, addition, adequate, ac-cede, af-fect, ag-gression, an-nihilate, ap-point, ar-rogant, as-sent, at-tract, ac-quiesce* + *adfix, adrenal.*
Ambi 'round about, on both sides, of two kinds,' prep.: *ambidextrous, amb-ition, amb-iguity, am-putate* + *ambigenous.*
Ante 'before,' prep.: *antepenult, antecedent* + *ante-bellum.*
Bene 'well,' adv.: *benediction, benefit, benevolence.*

Bi 'two, doubly,' from *bis* 'twice,' adv.: *biceps, biennial, biped* + *biconvex* — *biweekly, bimonthly.*

Circum 'around,' prep.: *circumflex, circumscribe, circumnavigate, circu-it* + *circumpolar, circumcircle.*

Cis, citra 'on this side of,' prep.: *cisalpine* + *cisatlantic, citramontane.*

Com 'together, thoroughly,' prep.: *com-estibles, combine, command, conclude, conduct, conquest, contact, col-lect, cor-rupt, co-gnate, co-operate* + *coextensive* — *co-trustee.*

Contra 'against,' prep.: *contravene, contro-versy* + *counterfeit, counter-march.*

De 'from, down from,' prep.: *delegate, deny, degrade* + — *deflesh.*

Dis 'apart,' insep.: *dis-cern, dis-tract, di-rect* + *debar, decamp, defeat, des-cant, disbar* — *dislike.*

Ex 'out of, upwards, thoroughly,' prep.: *exasperate, exercise, exhaust, e-ducation, e-lect, e-numerate, ex-sert* and *ex-ert* (Latin *ex-sertus*), *ex-pect* (*ex-specto*) + *ex-senator* — *ex-queen.*

Extra 'outside, beyond,' prep.: *extramundane* + *extralegal.*

Foris 'outside,' adv.: + *forfeit, foreclose.*

In 'not,' insep.: *inelegant, infelicity, im-provident, insane, i-gnoble* + *insecure, ineludible.*

In 'in, into,' prep.: *initial, inure, incarnate, institute* + — *endear, embody.*

Infra 'below,' prep.: + *infra-human* — *infra-red.*

Inter 'between,' prep.: *intercede, interdict, interest, intel-lect* + *enterprise, entertain, intercostal, intercollegiate* — *interleaf, interlink.*

Intra 'within,' prep.: + *intramural, intracanonical, intraglobular.*

Intro 'within,' adv.: *introduce, introspection* + *introvert, introthoracic.*

Juxta 'near,' prep.: + *juxtapose, juxtaposition, juxtamarine.*

Male 'ill,' adv.: *malediction, malefactor, malevolent.*

Minus 'less,' adv.: + *misrule, misuse.*

Non 'not,' adv.: + *non-conductor, non-combatant, nondescript, nonentity, non-suit.*

Ob 'towards, against,' prep.: *oblige, obstacle, obdurate, obviate, oc-casion, of-fer, op-press, obs-cene, os-tentation, o-mit* + *obovate, obcordate.*

Per 'through, thoroughly,' prep.: *perplex, perennial, perceive, percussion, pel-lucid* + *par-don, perforce, peroxide* — *per-haps.*

Post 'after,' prep.: *postpone, postscript* + *postdate, post-exilic.*

Prae 'before,' prep.: *precise, precept, prefer* + *preëxcellent, preavowal, pre-Victorian.*

Praeter, 'beyond,' prep.: *preterit, pretermit* + *preternatural.*

Pro 'before, forth, in behalf of,' prep.: *protest, proportion, pronoun, proconsul, prod-igy, prod-igal.*

Re 'back, against, again,' insep.: *refuge, resolve, red-olent* + *reagent.*

Retro 'backward,' adv.: *retroactive, retrocede, retrograde* + *retrorenal, retroject.*

Se 'apart,' insep.: *sed-ition, secede, se-cure, secret, seclude, se-dulous, segregate, select:* unproductive in English.

Semi 'half,' insep.: *semicircle, semiannual* + *semicolon, semicentennial, semi-anthracite.*

Sub 'under,' prep.: *subdivide, submerge, subvert* + *submarine, sublease, subclass.*

Subter 'beneath,' prep.: *subterfuge* + *subterhuman.*

Super 'over, above,' prep.: *superficial, supercilious* + *supernatural* — *supersix.*

Supra 'over, above, beyond,' prep.: + *supra-auricular, supraclavicle.*

Trans 'across, beyond,' prep.: *transact, transalpine, transfer, tran-scend, tran-scribe, tra-dition, tra-verse* + *transfrontal* — *transship.*

Ultra 'beyond,' prep.: *ultramundane* + *ultramarine, ultraviolet.*

Vice 'in the place of,' ablative case of a defective noun: + *vicegerent, vice-chancellor, vis-count.*

Prefixes of Greek origin, found in English words:

A or *an* 'not,' insep.: *achromatic, an-aemia, an-aesthetic, anonymous.*

Amphi 'round about, on both sides, of two kinds,' prep.: *amphibious, amphitheater.*

Ana 'up, according to,' prep.: *Anabaptist, anabasis, anachronism, analogy, anatomy.*

Anti 'against,' prep.: *antidote, antiphon, anti-Christ, ant-agonist, ant-arctic, ant-helion* + *anti-imperialism, antitoxin, antipodes.*

Apo 'from, away,' prep.: *apocalypse, apocrypha, apodosis, apology, ap-helion.*

Cata 'down, against,' prep.: *catacomb, catapult, catalogue, cataract, cat-hode, cat-holic.*

Di 'twice,' from adv. δίς: *dilemma, dissyllable* (which has assumed an extra *s*).

Dia 'through,' prep.: *diabolical, diadem, diagonal, dialogue, diagram* + *di-orama.*

Dys 'ill,' insep.: *dyspepsia, dysentery.*

En 'in,' prep.: *encomium, encyclical, encyclopaedia, encaustic, emblem, empirical, empyrean, el-lipse.* Also *endo* 'within,' from a prep.: + *endogen, endocarp, endogamy.*

Epi 'on, beside, above,' prep.: *epidermis, episcopal, epigram, epitaph, epiphany, ep-och, ep-hemeral.*

Ex 'out of,' prep.: *exegesis, ec-centric, ec-clesiastical, ec-zema.* Also *exo,* prep., and *ecto,* from a prep., 'outside': + *exocarp, exogen, exoskeleton, ectocardia.*

Hyper 'over, above,' prep.: *hyperbola, hypercritical, hyperbaton, hypermetrical* + *hyperacid.*

Hypo 'under,' prep.: *hypocrisy, hypochondriac, hypothesis, hyp-hen* ('under one').

Meta 'with, after,' prep.: *metaphor, metamorphosis, met-onymy, met-hod.*

Para 'alongside, over against,' prep.: *parable, paradox, parasite, paradigm, par-allel, par-enthesis, par-oxysm, par-ody, parish.*

Peri 'round about,' prep.: *perimeter, period, peripatetic* + *periscope, pericardium, periosteal.*

Pro 'before,' prep.: *prologue, proboscis, problem, prognosis, prophet.*

Pros 'to, in addition to,' prep.: *proselyte, prosody.*

Syn 'with,' prep.: *synagogue, synod, synopsis, synthesis, sym-bol, symmetry, symphony, syl-logism, syl-lable, sy-stem.*

Native English Prefixes, still in living use; examples after the + sign were not used in Anglo-Saxon:

A in + *ashore, a-hunting — across; be* in *behind* + *bedim — because, betinged; fore* in *forehead* + *foreground — forecastle; in* in *inborn* + *inbred; mis* in *misdeed* + *misgiving; off* in *offspring* + *offhand — offcolor; on* in *onlooker* + *onward; out* in *outward, outlaw* + *outbid — outdistance; over* in *oversee* + *overalls — overarch; un* in *unshorn* + *ungodly — unjust; un* in *unlock* + *unload — unline; under* in *understand* + *underdo — undercharge; up* in *upland, upright* + *upset, uphill — upturned.*

16. Other Latin suffixes forming abstracts, but not productive in English: *or* in *honor, favor, labor; tura* or *sura* in *nature, curvature, aperture, pressure; atus* (fifth declension) in *consulate, episcopate; men* in *specimen, legume, germ.* Also Greek *ma,* in *drama, comma, problem, stratagem, scheme, theme.*

17. A similar neuter ending *ium* was present in the Latin originals of *equilibrium, college, silence, council, counsel, study.*

18. Latin words with the suffix *aris* give us *singular, familiar, peculiar;* this ending was in origin quite distinct from *arius,* but the two were confused even in Latin.

19. By a very early development of the sound, the *t* of the passive participle appeared in Latin as *s* in some words, especially if the stem to which the suffix was attached, ended in certain consonants. The same variation arises in certain other suffixes: *auditor* and *divisor, addition* and *division, nature* and *pressure, directory* and *illusory,* as well as the participial *complete* and *reverse.*

20. *Ilis,* with short *i,* formed verbal adjectives when attached to verbal stems, as in *fragile, agile,* or to participial stems, as in *sessile, reptile. Ilis,* with long *i,* made adjectives from substantive stems, as in *civil, hostile.* Neither of these was identical with the suffix *bilis,* and neither was productive in English.

21. Latin *inus,* with long *i,* is a similar suffix, seen in *divine, feminine, equine;* an identical Greek suffix is responsible for the ending of *elephantine, crystalline,* and the *ine* in chemical terms, such as *chlorine* and *bromine* (which may be written without the final *e*), and in medicines, such as *listerine.*

NOTES

22. Latin *idus* forms adjectives, chiefly denoting permanent qualities, as in *solid, fluid, timid;* they are often associated with abstracts ending in *or* (Note 16), as in *humor* and *humid, stupor* and *stupid, liquor* and *liquid.*

23. This is an adjectival *ius* attached to the *tor* or *sor* suffix: *peremptory, perfunctory, cursory, illusory;* the neuter is often used as a substantive, *natatorium, moratorium, directory.*

24. Other words with Latin *icus: aquatic, erratic, fanatic, lunatic, public, unique, savage* (from Latin *silvaticus*).

25. The Greek endings *ist, ism, ic* change the vowel to *a* if an *i* precedes: *enthusiast, enthusiasm, elegiac, cardiac. Maniac* gives *iac* to *golf·iac.* The same change is true of the patronymic ending *id*, which forms names of nymphs (*Nereid, Danaid, pleiad, naiad* — often transferred to constellations), of epic poems (*Iliad, Thebaid*, the Latin *Aeneid*, the French *Jeremiad*, the English *Dunciad*), of zoölogical families (*Felidae* 'cat family,' *Canidae* 'dog family').

26. Certain of these suffixes are given in Notes 16–25.

27. Cf. N. W. DeWitt, "On Making New Words," in *The Classical Weekly*, XV. 89–91 (1922).

28. Examples of Anglo-Saxon suffixes attached to Latin and Greek stems: *paint-er, point-er, marin-er; sack-ful, box-ful; tutor-ing, sign-ing, paint-ing; scarce-ness, immense-ness, plenteous-ness; priest-craft, state-craft; duke-dom, martyr-dom; false-hood, parent-hood; member-ship, scholar-ship, clerk-ship; Johnn-y, Bess-ie; flower-y, palm-y, savor-y; fever-ish, brut-ish, tiger-ish; use-less, art-less, count-less; court-ly* (adj.); *use-ful, art-ful, merci-ful; quarrel-some, cumber-some, venture-some; barb-ed, color-ed, turret-ed, arm-ed; church-ward, city-ward; million-th, billion-th; round-ly, rude-ly savage-ly* (adverbs); *cross-wise.*

29. Examples of Latin nominative singular forms appearing unchanged as English words; *indicates that the dictionaries (Webster's and Murray's) authorize only the Latin plural, ° shows that they authorize both the Latin plural and the English·plural in *s* or *es:*

Decl. I, fem.: *alumna*, antenna°, area°, arena, aurora, boa°, caesura°, cicada°, copula°, cornucopia, corolla, corona°, de-*

[167]

mentia, era, farina, formula°, inertia, insomnia, lacuna°, larva*, medulla, militia, nebula*, peninsula, penumbra*, pupa*, saliva, scintilla, sequela*, umbra*, verbena, vertebra°, villa; the Latin plural ends in *ae.*

Decl. II, masc. and fem.: *alumnus*, animus, arbutus, bacillus*, calculus°, campus, circus, cirrus*, convolvulus°, cumulus*, denarius*, famulus*, fasciculus*, fiscus, focus°, fungus°, genius°, gladiolus°, humus, incubus°, mucus, nimbus°, nucleolus°, nucleus°, radius°, stimulus*, terminus*, villus*;* the Latin plural ends in *i. Cancer, minister, vesper.* Neuter: *virus.*

Decl. II, neut.: *alluvium°, arboretum°, cerebrum°, cerebellum°, compendium°, consortium, curriculum°, delirium°, effluvium°, equilibrium°, exordium°, forum°, frustum°, fulcrum°, interregnum°, lustrum°, millennium°, momentum°, nasturtium, odium, opprobrium, pabulum, premium, simulacrum°, spectrum°, tedium, triennium*, velum*;* the Latin plural ends in *a.*

Adjectives, Decl. II and I, masc.: *bonus, emeritus*, quietus; conifer, integer, miser, pauper, sinister.* Fem.: *abscissa°, cornea, quadragesima, quinquagesima, sexagesima, rotunda, ultima, penultima, antipenultima.* Neut.: *aquarium°, auditorium°, columbarium*, herbarium°, honorarium°, moratorium*, natatorium*, sanatorium°, sanitarium°, scriptorium°, solarium*, vivarium°;* perf. pass. participles, *datum*, desideratum*, dictum°, erratum*, sanctum, sputum*, stratum°, ultimatum°;* gerundives, *addendum*, agendum*, corrigendum*, memorandum*; album, decorum, maximum°, medium°, minimum*, modicum, nostrum, pendulum, quantum*, serum°, trivium*, vacuum°;* Latin plurals as in nouns of the same endings.

Decl. III, masc. and fem.: *ardor, candor, clamor, color, error, favor, fervor, honor, horror, humor, languor, liquor, odor, pallor, rancor, rigor, rumor, savor, squalor, stupor, tenor, terror, torpor, tumor, valor, vapor, vigor; agitator, assessor, creator, divisor, doctor, equator, factor, generator, indicator, inventor, janitor, liberator, monitor, sculptor, ventilator,* and many others ending in *tor; administratrix*, cicatrix*, executrix°, imperatrix, inheritrix, proprietrix, prosecutrix*,* *testatrix*, with Latin plural in *ices; amanuensis*, axis**, with Latin plurals in *es; apex°, appendix°, codex*, ibex°, index°, matrix°, vertex°, vortex°*, with Latin plurals in *ices; crux°*, Latin plural *cruces; forceps°*, Latin plural *forcipes; consul, farrago, finis, frater, lens, lumbago, mater, pater, pollen, ratio, torpedo, tyro* or *tiro, virago, vireo.*

Decl. III, neut.: *genus°, opus**, Latin plural in *era; cognomen°, gravamen°*, Latin plural in *mina; abdomen, acumen, albumen, bitumen, omen, specimen, stamen, onus, animal, tribunal, sulphur, tuber.*

Decl. III, adj.: *anterior, excelsior, exterior, inferior, interior, junior, major, minor, posterior, prior, senior, superior, ulterior; minus, plus; simile, biceps, triceps, duplex, triplex, par, velox.*

Decl. IV: *apparatus°, census, consensus, excursus°, hiatus°, impetus, prospectus, sinus°, status**; the Latin plural is spelled like the singular.

Decl. V: *congeries*, rabies, scabies, series*, species°, superficies**; the Latin plural is the same as the singular.

30. *Extra* may be in reality a shortening of *extraordinary*, and not an independent use of the Latin word *extra*.

31. Examples of Greek nominatives retaining their endings in English, unchanged or Latinized; the plurals are indicated as in the preceding list:

Decl. I, fem.: *agape°, anastrophe, anemone, antistrophe, apocope, apostrophe, catastrophe, enallage, hypallage, hyperbole, strophe°, syncope, synecdoche, systole; acacia, ambrosia, amnesia, anaesthesia, camera°, clepsydra°, dyspepsia, encyclopaedia, magnesia, naphtha, nausea, onomatopoeia, orchestra, paronomasia, pharmacopoeia, pneumonia, sepia°, stoa;* with Latinized ending, *amoeba°, basilica°, drachma°, hepatica°, hyperbola, parabola, sciatica;* the Greek plural is Latinized to *ae.*

Decl. I, masc.: *diabetes, pyrites.*

Decl. II, masc. and fem.: *apoxyomenos, asbestos, diadumenos;* with Latinized ending, *carpus*, choragus*, crocus, discus°, eucalyptus°, exodus, hippopotamus°, iambus°, isthmus°,* *oesophagus, syllabus*°, *tarsus**, *typhus;* the Greek plural is Latinized to *i*.

Decl. II, neut.: *anacoluthon**, *anthelion**, *aphelion**, *asyndeton, automaton, colon*°, *electron, etymon*°, *lexicon, macron, moron, onomasticon, parergon**, *parhelion*°, *pentathlon**, *perihelion**, *phenomenon**, *propylon*°, *rhododendron*°*;* with Latinized ending, *asylum*°, *athenaeum*°, *cranium*°, *electrum, emporium*°, *encomium*°, *epithalamium*°, *geranium, gymnasium*°, *mausoleum*°, *museum*°, *odeum**, *opium, plectrum*°, *proœmium, proscenium**, *stadium*°, *symposium*°*;* the Greek plural ends in *a*.

Decl. III, masc. and fem.: *analysis, apodosis, apotheosis, basis, diaeresis, emphasis, exegesis, hypothesis, metamorphosis, metathesis, parenthesis, periphrasis, prophylaxis, protasis, synthesis, thesis,* all with the Latinized plural in *es,* so far as their meanings permit them to be used in the plural at all; *calyx*°, Greek plural in *ces; larynx**, *pharynx**, *phalanx*°, *sphinx*°, Greek plural in *ges; ibis*°, *iris*°, *proboscis*°, Greek plural in *ides; Cyclops*°, Greek plural *Cyclopes; octopus*°, Greek plural *octopodes,* wrongly formed Latin plural *octopi; climax, lynx, onyx, thorax, aegis, aeon* or *eon, canon, chameleon, cotyledon, crater, demon, ether, lichen, litotes, paean, panther, phaëton, polyhistor, rhinoceros, scazon, siren.*

Decl. III, neut.: *anathema*°, *aroma*°, *asthma, carcinoma**, *coma, comma*°, *cyclorama, dilemma, diorama, diploma*°, *dogma*°, *drama, enema*°, *enigma*°, *glaucoma, lemma*°, *panorama, stemma**, *stigma*°, *zeugma,* Greek plural in *mata; chaos, erysipelas, nectar, pancreas, kudos.*

32. See *Iliad,* I. 599.

33. Cf. *Revelation,* 1. 8, 11; 21. 6; 22. 13.

34. *Anti* may be merely a shortening of words like *antisuffragist,* rather than a direct use of the Greek preposition as an independent word in English; cf. p. 118, above.

35. Examples of English given names, taken from Latin and Greek without loss of the nominative ending:

From Latin: names of men, *Amandus, Amor, Augustus, Aurelius, Caesar, Cornelius, Felix, Julius, Lucius, Mar-*

cellus, Marcus, Rex, Rufus, Victor; names of women, *Alma, Amanda, Augusta, Aurora, Barbara, Carmen, Cecilia, Clara, Claudia, Constantia, Cornelia, Diana, Emilia, Flora, Julia, Lavinia, Letitia, Lucia, Marcella, Marcia, Minerva, Olivia, Patricia, Paula, Portia, Priscilla, Regina, Rosa, Sabina, Stella, Sylvia, Vera, Veronica, Vesta, Victoria, Viola, Virginia, Viva.*

From Greek: names of men, *Aeneas, Erasmus, Hector, Leo, Nicodemus, Philippus, Sparta, Theophilus, Ulysses;* names of women, *Agatha, Alethea, Anastasia, Athena, Berenice, Cora, Daphne, Dorcas, Doris, Dorothea, Eugenia, Helena, Iris, Lydia, Melissa, Pandora, Penelope, Phoebe, Rhea, Sibylla, Sophia, Thalia, Theodora, Zenobia, Zeta, Zoe.*

36. See *Iliad*, V. 785.

37. Many of these are printed in Keil's *Grammatici Latini*, 7 vols., Leipzig, 1855–1880.

38. The editions of 1527 and 1566 are reprinted in *Jahrb. d. deut. Shakespeare-Gesellschaft*, XLIV. 65–117 (1908) and XLV. 51–100 (1909).

39. A number of these have been edited and reprinted by R. Brotanek, *Neudrucke frühneuenglischer Grammatiken*, 8 vols., Halle, 1905–1913; some others are listed in the bibliography of Goold Brown's *Grammar of English Grammars* [10], New York, 1884.

40. An unreflective and unscholarly attitude toward our mother tongue has in recent years attempted to reduce formal English grammar virtually to the learning of some half dozen endings to be used in specific places (*'s, s, s'* in substantives, and *s, ed, ing* in verbs), and has greatly lowered the appreciation and the mastery of our English speech. We nowadays constantly find in writing or in print the errors illustrated in this sentence: *If I was there, I would tell he and she not to dare to say that it was me who is responsible.* Why?

41. Another striking instance of the importance of the Latin element is seen in the preamble to the Constitution of the United States, as follows, with the Latin words in italics: "We the *people* of the *United States*, in *order* to *form* a more *perfect Union*, *establish justice*, *insure domestic tranquillity*,

provide for the *common defense, promote* the *general* welfare and *secure* the blessings of *liberty* to ourselves and our *posterity,* do *ordain* and *establish* this *Constitution* for the *United States* of *America.*" The last word, *America,* is not an ancient Latin word, but a modern Latin word, made from the Italian name Amerigo.

42. *Educational Problems*, New York, 1911, II. 256–257.

BIBLIOGRAPHY

Those who are desirous of reading further on the topics discussed in this volume, are referred to the works cited in the notes, and to the following:

I. On Linguistics and on the History of the Languages:

JESPERSEN, OTTO, *Language, Its Nature, Development and Origin.* New York, 1922.

BENDER, H. H., *The Home of the Indo-Europeans.* Princeton, 1922.

STURTEVANT, E. H., *Linguistic Change.* Chicago, 1917.

Encyclopaedia Britannica [11], especially the articles on *Indo-European Languages, Greek Language, Latin Language, English Language.* Cambridge, England, 1910–1911.

GREENOUGH, J. B., and KITTREDGE, G. L., *Words and their Ways in English Speech;* Chapter VIII deals with *The Latin in English.* New York, 1901.

II. Grammars and Histories of the English Language, etc.:

BAUGH, A. C., *History of the English Language;* shortly to appear from the press of the Century Co., New York.

BRADLEY, HENRY, *The Making of English,* with a good appreciation of the Latin in English. New York, 1904.

EMERSON, O. F., *The History of the English Language.* New York, 1894.

GREEN, RUSSELL, *The Just Use of a Latin Element in English Style.* Oxford (The Chancellor's Essay), 1915.

JESPERSON, OTTO, *Growth and Structure of the English Language* [3]. Leipzig, 1912.

LOUNSBURY, T. R., *The History of the English Language* [2]. New York, 1894.

MEIKLEJOHN, J. M. D., *History of the English Language,* revised American edition. New York, 1909.

MORRIS, RICHARD, *Historical Outlines of English Accidence* [2], revised by L. Kellner and H. Bradley; Chapter IV and

Appendix III contain lists of words according to their appearance before or after the Norman Conquest, and according to their first appearance in specific authors. London and New York, 1895.

SKEAT, W. W., *Principles of English Etymology;* the first volume deals with the native element and the second volume with the foreign element. Oxford, 1887 and 1891.

TRENCH, R. C., *English Past and Present*, which first appeared in 1855, and has seen many revised editions since that date. London and New York.

III. On Words, Prefixes, and Suffixes:

BLACKBURN, E. M., *The Study of Words*. New York, 1911.

KELLOGG, B., and REED, A., *Word Building;* this consists chiefly of a list of roots, mostly of Latin or Greek origin, with prefixes and suffixes. New York, 1903.

MURRAY, J. A. H., *A New English Dictionary Based on Historical Principles*. Oxford, 1883–1923; now nearly complete.

SKEAT, W. W., *An Etymological Dictionary of the English Language*[4]. Oxford, 1910.

SKEAT, W. W., *A Concise Etymological Dictionary of the English Language*[2]. Oxford, 1901.

SKEAT, W. W., *Notes on English Etymology*. Oxford, 1901.

WEBSTER'S *New International Dictionary of the English Language*, edited by W. T. Harris and F. S. Allen. Springfield (Mass.), 1912.

WEEKLEY, E., *The Romance of Words*. New York, 1912.

WEEKLEY, E., *An Etymological Dictionary of Modern English*. New York, 1921.

The histories and grammars of English also contain chapters on prefixes and suffixes.

IV. On the Alphabet and Writing:

THOMPSON, E. M., *Handbook of Greek and Latin Palaeography;* this contains an account of the development of the various styles of writing. New York, 1893.

Encyclopaedia Britannica (see above), articles on *Alphabet*, on the various letters of the alphabet, on *Palaeography*.

MURRAY'S *New English Dictionary* (see above), articles on the letters of the alphabet.

Our Debt to Greece and Rome

AUTHORS AND TITLES

AUTHORS AND TITLES

HOMER. *John A. Scott.*

SAPPHO. *David M. Robinson.*

EURIPIDES. *F. L. Lucas.*

ARISTOPHANES. *Louis E. Lord.*

DEMOSTHENES. *Charles D. Adams.*

THE POETICS OF ARISTOTLE. *Lane Cooper.*

GREEK RHETORIC AND LITERARY CRITICISM. *W. Rhys Roberts.*

LUCIAN. *Francis G. Allinson.*

CICERO AND HIS INFLUENCE. *John C. Rolfe.*

CATULLUS. *Karl P. Harrington.*

LUCRETIUS AND HIS INFLUENCE. *George Depue Hadzsits.*

OVID. *Edward Kennard Rand.*

HORACE. *Grant Showerman.*

VIRGIL. *John William Mackail.*

SENECA THE PHILOSOPHER. *Richard Mott Gummere.*

APULEIUS. *Elizabeth Hazelton Haight.*

MARTIAL. *Paul Nixon.*

PLATONISM. *Alfred Edward Taylor.*

ARISTOTELIANISM. *John L. Stocks.*

STOICISM. *Robert Mark Wenley.*

LANGUAGE AND PHILOLOGY. *Roland G. Kent.*

AUTHORS AND TITLES

Aeschylus and Sophocles. *J. T. Sheppard.*

Greek Religion. *Walter Woodburn Hyde.*

Survivals of Roman Religion. *Gordon J. Laing.*

Mythology. *Jane Ellen Harrison.*

Ancient Beliefs in The Immortality of The Soul. *Clifford H. Moore.*

Stage Antiquities. *James Turney Allen.*

Plautus and Terence. *Gilbert Norwood.*

Roman Politics. *Frank Frost Abbott.*

Psychology, Ancient and Modern. ' *G. S. Brett.*

Ancient and Modern Rome. *Rodolfo Lanciani.*

Warfare by Land and Sea. *Eugene S. McCartney.*

The Greek Fathers. *James Marshall Campbell.*

Greek Biology and Medicine. *Henry Osborn Taylor.*

Mathematics. *David Eugene Smith.*

Love of Nature among the Greeks and Romans. *H. R. Fairclough.*

Ancient Writing and its Influence. *B. L. Ullman.*

Greek Art. *Arthur Fairbanks.*

Architecture. *Alfred M. Brooks.*

Engineering. *Alexander P. Gest.*

Modern Traits in Old Greek Life. *Charles Burton Gulick.*

Roman Private Life. *Walton Brooks McDaniel.*

Greek and Roman Folklore. *William Reginald Halliday.*

Ancient Education. *J. F. Dobson.*